LOCAL GOVERNMENT

ITS ROLE AND FUNCTION

**Steve Leach and Murray Stewart with
Howard Davies and Christine Lambert**

JR
JOSEPH
ROWNTREE
FOUNDATION

Published by
Joseph Rowntree Foundation
The Homestead
40 Water End
York YO3 6LP

Tel: (0904) 629241

ISBN 1 872470 55 6

Designed by Peter Adkins Design

Printed in Great Britain by Colour Spec., Beverley

LOCAL GOVERNMENT

ITS ROLE AND FUNCTION

CONTENTS

ACKNOWLEDGEMENTS

This study was undertaken as part of the Joseph Rowntree Foundation's Local and Central Government Research Programme. The team from INLOGOV and SAUS was led by Steve Leach and Murray Stewart with Howard Davies and Christine Lambert. It involved a wide range of colleagues from both institutions as well as from the Universities of Glasgow and Ulster. These colleagues include Sally Burrell, Paul Burton, Michael Connolly, Andrew Coulson, Adrian Franklin, Colin Fudge, John Gibson, Julian le Grand, Robin Hambleton, Lesley Hoyes, Gervase Huxley, Martin Loughlin, Barrie Loveday, Philip Nanton, Phyllida Parsloe, Kathryn Riley, Chris Skelcher, Kieron Walsh and Matthew Warburton.

INTRODUCTION

The background

The last decade has seen a stream of legislation altering both the formal powers and duties laid by Parliament on local authorities and the more informal balance of power between centre and periphery. There has been manifest conflict between Whitehall and local government and an explicit effort by the centre to shift the culture of local government from what was seen as bureaucratic and monopolistic provision to a new 'enabling' role. Privatisation, CCT, and the reform of education, housing and social services have demanded a revision of attitudes to service planning and provision.

Alongside this turbulent legal environment has been a shift in the external environment. The spread of European Commission influence has altered the role and function of local authorities, particularly in the environmental and consumer protection fields; the impact of economic restructuring, recovery, and recession has forced a reappraisal of local approaches to economic development and urban regeneration; new approaches to leisure and the arts have brought fresh challenges; recognition - from right and left - of the responsibility of the public sector to consumer and citizen has led to radical ideas about forms of service delivery, responsiveness and quality in public service provision.

Above all 1991 has offered an official review by central government of the finance and structure of local government with local taxation, the structure of local government, and internal management all explicitly on the political agenda. Three consultation papers on these issues have been published and further changes in the arrangements for government at the local level are inevitable.

In 1990 the Joseph Rowntree Foundation commissioned from the Institute of Local Government Studies (University of Birmingham) and the School for Advanced Urban Studies (University of Bristol) a study of the role and function of local government. The INLOGOV/SAUS team included colleagues from the Universities of Glasgow and Ulster.

The method of research proposed by the team and accepted by the Foundation did not involve the collection of extensive new information about what local government does. Instead the resources of the two institutions were used to reflect on the experience of the last decade and to develop an overview of the role and function of local government as a whole at the beginning of the 1990s. The specific method of working involved three elements:

(i) an overview of the full range of local government services and functions to provide an assessment of the changing patterns of formal discretion and control.

(ii) case studies of a number of key service areas and functions selected to illustrate differing aspects of contemporary role and function. These case studies covered a number of services (for example, education), cross-cutting areas of service activity (for example, urban regeneration), functions (for example, planning). Additional work was done on other key topics (for example, community and locality). In each case study research interviews were carried out with a range of relevant organisations (mainly local authorities, but where appropriate central government departments, professional associations and local authority associations). Three 'core authorities' (Gloucestershire, Cheltenham, Wolverhampton) were visited in the majority of case studies.

The topics covered in the case studies were:

Services
    Education
    Housing
    Libraries and arts
    The fire service
    Waste management
    Economic development and tourism

Cross-cutting service structures
    Local government services for older people
    Urban regeneration
    Play

Functions
    Strategic planning and structure planning
    Resource acquisition
    The decentralisation of council services
    Grant aid
    Contracts, competition and public service
    Accountability mechanisms in the local government system

Other background work was carried out on local government in Northern Ireland, community and locality, area and power, and local government and quasi-markets.

(iii) the synthesis of the above material into a final review of the role and function of local government. This involved the development of arguments about the changing nature of discretion and political control in the light of changes within the different areas of service responsibility. This report is the output from this overall review of role and function.

The remainder of this introduction provides a brief set of concepts and definitions to assist interpretation of the subsequent more substantive sections of the report. Chapter 1 covers the functions of local government and is directed to a discussion of service responsibilities followed by an exploration of the functions of local government distinguishing between eight functions - direct service provision, service purchasing, regulation, facilitation, planning, resource acquisition and allocation, organisation, and accountability.

Chapter 2 provides a set of models or ideal types against which different expressions of role and function can be assessed and evaluated. Finally Chapter 3 discusses the practical implications of the 'ideal type' analysis for future directions in thinking about systems and structures of local government.

Concepts and definitions
The almost unprecedented weight and pace of the change experienced by local government in the last decade (and even before), has given rise to an inconsistent set of assumptions about role and function. This research examines, on a service-by-service and function-by-function basis, the impact of recent changes on

two key dimensions of local government activity: the extent and use of local discretion and the extent and operation of local political choice and control. The two factors are of course inter-related. Areas of local discretion in the provision of services may be exploited by local elected members in terms of their political (or other) values. Alternatively discretion and control may, in the absence of member input, be exploited by officers, or on occasion not recognised at all. Indeed there is a possible position in which members (or officers) perceive and exercise an area of discretion which is subsequently shown to be illegitimate.

Discretion

This can be defined in a number of ways:

(i) Policy discretion - in relation to the scope and content of local policies and service-provision recognising that some activities are mandatory whilst others are permissive.

(ii) Financial discretion - in relation to resource acquisition and allocation, including discretion to generate resources and discretion regarding allocation amongst different services.

(iii) Service delivery discretion - in the mode of organisation and form of provision of services (for example, contracting, decentralisation).

(iv) Administrative discretion - in the implementation of policies in terms of the administrative and professional norms and procedures of those with executive responsibility.

(v) Political discretion - to take political decisions about policy, finance, or service delivery within the limits of the legislative framework.

The scope for political control is directly related to the scope for discretion within the local government system. The distinction has been made between:

• the councillor's role as an elected representative for a small area (ward or neighbourhood), with a concern for the interests of that area and those who live in it (within which case-worker and local advocate roles may be found)

• the councillor's role as an elected representative for the authority as a whole and the communities it represents (for example, political activist; external advocate/networker)

- the councillor's role as a member of the council for the policies of the authority and their effective administration/implementation (for example, strategist, service policy, service administration)

- the councillor's role as a member of the council for the effective working of the organisation (for example, strategic management).

The first two of these roles are manifestations of the councillor's representative responsibilities, whilst the last two reflect their organisational responsibilities. The two are clearly linked. In the past, the way local authorities have operated has given much more emphasis to councillors' organisational responsibilities as compared to their representative responsibilities.

The role and function of local government

A further set of conceptual distinctions are those used to identify the different levels of choice about future systems of local government with which the research project is concerned. Distinctions were made between the purposes, roles, functions, responsibilities and structures of local government, in the following terms:

- by purposes are meant the basic reasons, in the last decade of the century, for having local government at all. Examination of role and function is only meaningful in a context within which basic purpose is reassessed

- by roles (of local government) are meant the way in which its basic purposes are expressed institutionally, and the particular part which local government plays within the wider structure of government (for example, agent, provider, enabler, regulator)

- by functions are meant the modes of action through which local government seeks, or is allowed, to fulfil its role(s) (for example, planning, direct provision, purchasing, inspection, review)

- by service responsibilities are meant the service areas within which local government has a power or duty to operate (for example, housing, education, social services, but also cross-service responsibilities such as urban regeneration or community care)

- by structures are meant the ways government as a whole is organised (tiers and levels) as well as the ways in which individual local authorities exercise their discretion to plan, arrange, provide and control services.

The relationship between these concepts can be illustrated diagrammatically as follows:

DIAGRAM 1 - The Hierarchy of Levels of Analysis

Purposes of Local Government

Roles of Local Government

Service Responsibilities   **Functional Patterns**

Structure   **Finance**

Thus the set of assumptions adopted by the research (and reflected in the structure of this report) can be summarised as follows. The only way to resolve the uncertainty which exists about the future direction of local government is to start by clarifying what the fundamental purposes of local government are. Different conceptions about the basic purposes of local government imply differing interpretations of role. Such different roles in turn imply differing levels of emphasis on market and non-market forces with respect to the provision and distribution of public goods, and different levels of emphasis on the values of local autonomy / discretion in the provision of services and of community governance. These alternative emphases in turn suggest a different set of appropriate service responsibilities for local government, a different hierarchy of functions, and different organisational structures and financial arrangements. This report addresses primarily the middle two levels of this hierarchy - the role of local government, and service responsibilities and functional patterns.

The main aim of this report is to provide a framework for helping to resolve the current confusion and inconsistency about the interrelationship between the levels and to support the development of a robust and consistent system of sub-national government.

CHAPTER 1

THE FUNCTIONS OF LOCAL GOVERNMENT

Service responsibilities

In discussing local government it is normal to start with an analysis of service responsibilities - education, economic development, police, libraries and so on. Services can be categorised in a number of ways. Most recently, and as part of the Joseph Rowntree Foundation's Local and Central Government Relations Research Programme, Coopers and Lybrand Deloitte have suggested a categorisation of services in terms of need, protective, amenity and facility services. In this they adapt and extend the more traditional categorisation of need (or personal) services, infrastructure services and protective services.

Even a brief analysis of the changing nature of duties and powers shows, however, that analysis of role and function solely in terms of categories of services is inappropriate. Firstly, areas of service responsibility cannot be simply allocated to one or other category. In terms of the Coopers grouping, for example, social services involves need services (mental handicap), protective services (child abuse protection) and amenity (debt advice). The police service whilst dominated by its protective functions has an important amenity and facility role in relation to community policing and crime prevention. Economic development can involve a range of facilities and amenities as well as falling within the traditional infrastructure service band.

Secondly, many of the newer responsibilities of local government overlap between the traditional categories of services; environmental responsibilities are both 'protective' and 'amenity' in their characteristics, as indeed are the new litter responsibilities. Urban regeneration cuts across categories as do services to groups of people (older people or under-5s), or services to areas such as community development. Many of the equal opportunity initiatives taken by local authorities are significant by virtue of the fact that they cross service or departmental boundaries. Thus our work confirms that simple reference to services such as education, the police or fire as if the services were homogeneous in terms of the nature of the functions involved is misleading and naive. This is particularly the case when whole service areas (or what purport to be service areas) are discussed in terms of whether they should or should not be within the competence of local government.

Thirdly, local government cannot be seen simply as a system for the delivery of discrete services; the essence of local authorities is their potential to bring together services at the local level in the light of local needs and demands. It is the cumulative and aggregate impact of services which is the test of good local government.

Our research confirms the variety of activity within service areas in reflection of the fact that parts of a service (and in recent years a growing proportion) are subject to high degrees of central control, whereas other parts of what are often defined as the same service are in practice open to local discretion over the extent and method of implementation. Assessment of the extent of that local discretion and control is at the heart of this study.

The starting point for our analysis, therefore, is less a categorisation of services and more a concern for how local authorities exercise their service responsibilities. The key question is about functions - the modes of action through which local government seeks, or is allowed, to pursue its role.

Functional activities

There has been a major switch in relation to many of the service responsibilities of local government from an emphasis on 'direct provision' to an emphasis on 'enabling' (i.e. ensuring that a service is provided and regulated rather than providing it directly).

However, the pattern of change in local government responsibilities and functions over the past decade has been much more complex than a simple switch from provision to enabling, and this chapter illustrates the changing pattern of functions in local government showing how these changes have affected the capacity of local government to operate as an organ of community governance as opposed to an agency for providing a range of discrete services.

Eight important functions of local government are identified in Diagram 2. A distinction is made in the diagram between those functions which are concerned (in the broadest sense) with the basis of the provision of services of various kinds to the public, and those functions which are concerned with how local authorities organise and interrelate such service provision.

DIAGRAM 2
Direct and Indirect Functions of Local Government

PRIMARY FUNCTIONS	SECONDARY FUNCTIONS
Service Provision	**Planning**
	Strategic Planning
	Service Planning
	Structure Planning
Service Purchaser	**Resource Acquisition**
Specification	Budgeting
Contracting	Charge-setting
Monitoring	Charging
	Distribution
Regulation	**Organisation**
Inspection	Structure and Process
	Committees
Enforcement	Departments
Control	Area Basis
Facilitation	**Accountability and Review**
Grants and loans	Political Accountability
Advocacy	Market Accountability
Bargaining and Negotiation	Administrative Accountability
Promotion	Financial Accountability

The basis of provision can be arranged in (at least) four different ways:

direct service provision (of public housing, residential care, a library);

service purchasing (payment on a contractual basis to another organisation to provide the service, for example, employing a contractor to collect household waste);

regulation (of the economic behaviour of individuals or other agencies in the public interest by insisting that standards, rules and procedures of various kinds for exchange or provision of goods and services are complied with);

facilitation (persuasion of one or more other organisations to carry out activities which are judged to benefit the local community (e.g. by incentive through grants to voluntary organisations or loans to small businesses, or through processes of bargaining, persuasion, promotion or advocacy).

These are referred to as the primary functions of local government. Their separation into four distinct categories reflects (but avoids) the widespread use of the term 'enabling' which has been applied indiscriminately to what are in fact different functional roles of purchaser, facilitator and regulator functions.

There also exist four secondary functions which are concerned more with the way in which local authorities organise their business:

planning - many of the primary functions identified above are predicated on the basis of a longer-term strategic or service plan;

resource acquisition and allocation: local authorities have to acquire resources, and having acquired them, develop processes for allocating them amongst alternative uses;

internal organisation, including the chosen structure of Committees and Departments, but specifically in this report the extent of decentralisation to area-based structures of resource allocation, decision making and service delivery;

accountability and review: as a public agency, a local authority is accountable to the electorate, to users, and to central government and to the courts both for its expenditure and for the way it provides and distributes services.

All the functions identified - primary and secondary - are subject to a balance between central control and local discretion. For example, the curriculum to be taught in local authority schools may (or may not) be specified by central government; various services may be required to be purchased rather than provided directly; the scope for facilitation may be regulated by the government (see for example, the Part III provisions on economic development activities in the 1989 Local Government and Housing Act); the basis on which regulation of private sector (or individual) behaviour is carried out locally is often heavily circumscribed by the centre (various planning acts, regulations and circulars).

Similarly, in relation to the indirect functions identified, central government may require, in certain circumstances, the decentralisation of service provision within local government (for example, the local management of schools provisions of the 1988 Education Act), require that certain types of plan be produced (Structure Plans, HIPs), limit the scope for resource acquisition and allocation (through capping or ring-fencing), or require local authorities to undertake certain forms of accountability and review processes (external audit, elections, appeals).

The remainder of this section provides a brief review of each of the eight functions identified (five of which - planning, resource acquisition, service purchaser, organisation, and accountability and review - were the subject of specific case studies).

Service provision
In most areas of local authority service responsibility traditional practice has been for authorities to provide the service concerned directly (i.e. through their own organisation). Now, however, even where the local authority DLO or DSO has won the contract concerned, the internal relationship between client unit (or purchaser) and the provider has been transformed by the

requirement to compete, and by the subsequent existence of a contractual relationship between purchaser and provider. Since many DLOs and DSOs operate in effect as 'arms-length' companies within the local authority, the concept of 'direct service provision' is scarcely appropriate even where services are provided in-house.

However, it is not just in relation to the CCT legislation, but additionally in housing, education, and services for older people, that the local authority's direct service provision function has been affected. The provisions of the 1990 National Health and Community Care Act make it financially advantageous for local authorities to become service purchasers, rather than direct providers, of residential accommodation for the elderly (indeed some local authorities are in anticipation of the Act's implementation beginning to set up 'arms-length companies' for the purpose). The local management of schools (LMS) provisions of the 1988 Education Act similarly diminish the local authority's direct provision function and move authorities instead towards an emphasis on funding/purchasing and regulation. Proposals to remove colleges (and perhaps inspection and advice) from local authority control take the process further. The opting-out provisions of the 1987 Housing Act and the 1988 Education Act, insofar as they have been taken up, have further diluted the local authority's direct provision role. Thus the common themes of each of the major pieces of local government related legislation since 1987 has been to reduce the direct provision function of local councils and re-channel their energies towards purchasing and regulation. This research inevitably merely confirms this well-known trend but adds to the analysis in two particular ways.

First, our case study visits confirmed the emergence of 'new' areas of service responsibility. Local councillors have begun to shift their energies from traditional services to areas where there appears to be scope for an expanded provision role. Recreation and leisure in particular, cultural activity and the arts, and 'green' policies and programmes, in conjunction with other already established areas such as economic development and consumer protection have begun to offer members in particular a greater potential in what they see as direct service provision as a substitute for education, social services and housing.

Secondly, even in traditional service areas there remains scope for direct provision either in relation to local implementation where members can have a significant role or in the provision of specialist services which cannot be contracted out. Equally there is an increasing emphasis upon service integration - between housing and social services for example - as well as upon decentralised service delivery.

Service purchasing

The increasing emphasis on the function of 'service purchaser' - the specification and subsequent purchase of a service through the agreement of a contract - has probably been the most important change in functional emphasis which has occurred within local government over the past decade. Although local authorities have been free to put almost any service they are responsible for providing out to tender, it is only in the 1980s that legislation has *required* local authorities to go through a tendering process for certain specified services. Previously local authorities' use of contracting has been concentrated in construction projects and to a lesser degree (and much more selectively) in refuse collection, leisure, catering and car park management. Part III of the Local Government Planning and Land Act 1980 required authorities, if they wished to perform building and highway construction and maintenance work by direct labour, first to submit it to a tender process. The Transport Act of 1988 required local authorities to transfer bus undertakings into companies (which were mainly local authority owned). And, most importantly, the 1988 Local Government Act extended the contracting requirement to refuse collection, street cleaning, building cleaning, schools, welfare and other catering, vehicle maintenance, grounds maintenance and leisure management. The Education Reform Act of 1988 gives schools the right to let their own contracts for cleaning and grounds maintenance if they wish (and for catering, subject to certain conditions). The government has also stated its intention to require competition for waste disposal and has commended its value in relation to care services for the elderly.

Thus the local authority service purchaser role has been

extended over the decade to cover an increasingly wide range of services. Even when internal DLO or DSO units have won the contracts concerned (and most contracts under the 1988 Act have been won in-house), the change has clearly had a profound affect on the operations of local authorities through the separating out of purchaser and provider roles and the 'arms-length' status of the 'contracting units' concerned although the organisational clarity of this separation varies. The change has contributed materially to the fragmentation of the operations of local authorities and to major changes in organisational culture. It has resulted, for example (in increasing numbers of authorities) in a situation in which a wide range of internal local authority services (for example, computing, architectural design, quality surveying) have been defined on an internal contractor basis, with their services purchased or not by other local authority departments (for example, education, social services) on a service-level agreement or fee-paying basis. The move toward a strong service-purchaser function has thus had a more profound impact than the legislative provisions, far-reaching though they are, would suggest.

Regulation

The regulatory function of local government, which incorporates the more pro-active roles of inspection and enforcement as well as the more responsive activity of regulation itself, provided the major source of justification and legitimacy for the emerging local government system in the mid-nineteenth century. It has remained an important function within local government since and holds an importance which is inversely related to the role of direct provision by local government itself. Thus with the emergence of market mechanisms for local service provision regulation regains a pre-eminent position.

The regulatory function has always dominated the service responsibilities of environmental health and trading standards (including consumer protection and licensing) but has also been strong within town and country planning (development control, building control, conservation, listed buildings, tree preservation orders), waste disposal (site licensing, special waste regulations) and highways (access to highways, traffic management etc.).

Police is by definition a primarily regulatory activity in rather a different sense. Social services, particularly in relation to children at risk, have an important regulatory role, which has been broadened under the Children Act. The key distinction in the regulatory function is between standard-setting which is normally done nationally, and verification, inspection and enforcement which are done locally, and although by their very nature rule-bound, are in practice susceptible to variation in implementation (via the administrative discretion which exists in all services).

The regulatory function is already increasing in significance and is likely to continue to do so, for two reasons. First of all, the increasing number of EC Directives, in particular in relation to trading standards, environmental health and environmental concerns more generally, are likely to strengthen the range of responsibilities attached to the regulatory function in local government. Secondly, the increasing emphasis on the use of external agencies to provide services which are the formal responsibility of local authorities (i.e. the purchaser/provider distinction discussed earlier) will inevitably strengthen the local authority's regulatory role. The process of contract monitoring and enforcement is of course itself a form of regulation. In social services, the regulatory function has been considerably strengthened in the new arrangements which follow from the 1990 Community Care and Health Act.

> "the new community care legislation requires the setting-up of inspection units. These will take over from the existing units which are concerned with the registration of private care homes, but will have much wider scope. They will inspect not only private and voluntary residential care homes, but also such homes run by social services departments ..."

As the direct provision function in local government is reduced, so by implication is its regulatory role strengthened. The extent to which such enhanced regulation is felt to be necessary reflects, however, the extent to which the market (or voluntary bodies) are viewed as 'trustworthy' - i.e. as having the capacity and motivation for self-regulation. The regulatory role is given relatively little emphasis by the Adam Smith Institute, for example, despite the strong 'market emphasis' of their proposals for local government, but regulation is increasingly important in service areas affected by European legislation, notably in food and consumer protection.

There is no guarantee in the emphasis on the benefits of the market which currently pervade local government's operations that the increased regulatory role implied will necessarily be undertaken directly by local authorities themselves. An education authority visited during the research observed in relation to LEA inspectors (in terms which have become even more relevant since the field work was completed):

> "The implications for the Inspectorate are potentially immense. By 1992 they will have to be operating all their work according to clear service level agreements, and these agreements will be funded from funds devolved to institutions (with whom the agreement will be) or funds held by the LEA strategy group. Nowhere will there be a requirement to use the LEA Inspectorate. The Inspectorate will be 'out in the market'."

The principles behind this authority's view of school inspection could be extended to a wide range of other regulatory activities, either through legislation or through local authority choice and it is clear that the Education and Social Services Inspectorates are likely to become more significant whether provision is on a market or a different basis. Possibilities include a Quality Commission, an extended role for the Audit Commission, and the emergence of further institutional forms of inspection and account outside local government.

The regulatory function has never been one which offers much scope for local political discretion and control and may indeed offer even less in future. In relation to consumer protection the emphasis on quality control inspection and enforcement has shifted from the point of consumption towards the point of production and in consequence the local government role is moving from consumer protection to producer regulation, with implications of a possible decline in member involvement. Certainly European experience does not suggest that regulation-dominated services such as trading standards and environmental health are ones which require the exercise of strong local democratic control for their implementation.

Facilitation

The facilitation function (in its widest sense) of local government is one which has been developing an increasingly high profile in the 1980s, albeit on a very uneven basis (between authorities). It has been a key function of certain services for some time. Land-use planning has facilitated housing and industrial development; economic development activity has facilitated investment and job creation; in urban regeneration, tourism, and the arts some local authorities have a long tradition of bringing about change rather than doing it themselves; grant aid to the voluntary sector has long been used as a vehicle for facilitating non-statutory community development. Facilitation is becoming an increasingly important function within more traditional service responsibilities such as housing and social services. It is the function most closely associated with the more pro-active definition of the enabling activity (i.e. an emphasis on the wider concept of making things happen that would not otherwise do so, rather than the narrower contracting-out emphasis).

To some extent this pro-active facilitation role has been encouraged by central government (see Part III of 1989 Local Government and Housing Act), but in other ways limits have been set on the scope of local authority action in this field. The main themes in the development of urban regeneration policy and practice have been the growing centralisation of the policy, as evidenced by the proliferation of central initiatives and the growing presence of private sector interests within the policy. Most recently, however, there has been some rehabilitation of the local authority facilitating function as exemplified by the City Challenge experience

The Audit Commission has described the present institutional arrangements for facilitating local economic development as 'a patchwork quilt of complexity and idiosyncrasy' and argues that 'local authorities are the agents most likely to be able to take the lead in planning the future prosperity of their areas', whilst recognising the disparity of attitudes and approaches currently adopted within local government.

In the field of development/regeneration, therefore, an increased (but increasingly circumscribed) emphasis in local authorities on the pro-active enabler function can be identified. The same argument could be made in relation to grant aid - the provision of financial support for organisations which are neither public nor private and whose activities are carried out 'not for profit'. Although many authorities are predisposed to strengthen their 'pro-active facilitation' function in this respect, grant aid is an area of activity which is being increasingly threatened (in terms of the level of financial assistance involved) by the pressure on local authority revenue budgets generated by the new local government finance system.

In particular, in relation to social services, where there has long been a policy of enabling voluntary organisations to offer services which the local authority would have difficulty in providing there is now a contradiction. Voluntary groups are experiencing cuts in local authority funding whilst on the other hand central government policy is placing an increasing emphasis upon the enabling role of social service departments.

The facilitation function can be seen as a corollary of the strategic function (see below) in two ways: first, as an alternative to direct provision (in those areas of service responsibility not subject to CCT) where the local authority, having determined its strategy (for example, for housing, social services or economic development) promotes or facilitates the achievement of that strategy through external agencies; and secondly as a means through which the local authority's concern about major changes in its area that it cannot directly control (for example, the closure of a hospital) can be expressed, through advocacy, publicity or negotiation. Both aspects have increased in significance in recent years.

It is within their facilitating role that many local authorities are increasingly seeking to innovate. Evidence on play (in a case study for this project supported by the National Childrens' Play and Recreational Unit) as well as on greening and grant aid offer evidence of the different ways in which interdepartmental and inter-organisational approaches are being initiated and led by local authorities. Much of the running on European issues is being made by local authorities which in general have adapted faster than central government in accommodating at the local level to the pressures of change in Europe (trading standards on the one hand and the exploitation of the structural funds on the other being examples).

Secondary functions
Planning (strategic and service)

A striking feature of change is the increasing attention being paid by local authorities (particularly in England) to strategic or authority-wide planning. This is despite the lack of any legal requirement or government exhortation to do so (although strategic planning is a key feature of the local authority management processes recommended by the Audit Commission). What is involved is an explicit attempt to set out some kind of long-term strategic direction for a local authority either in terms of core values (responsiveness to the customer) or substantive priorities (strengthening the competitive position of a local centre) or both. This represents a major change in functional orientation in local government. The strategic approach is in part a response to the fragmentary impact of the Government's recent legislative programme, which has caused widespread recognition that if a local authority wants to retain a corporate identity (and a sense of being a governmental institution as opposed to the provider/purchaser of a set of discrete services) it needs to develop the strategic function. In part also strategic planning is required in order to shape the authority's response to resource constraints and uncertainty.

In the strategic statements produced by local authorities it is rare for some kind of objective or set of objectives about economic development not to figure prominently. In many areas and in particular in the declining industrial areas and cities outside the South East, there is likely to be a perception that the encouragement of economic development (or urban regeneration) should be a key element of an authority-wide strategy.

As well as the Audit Commission, the CBI has criticised the short-term and *ad hoc* nature of much urban regeneration work and advocated the development of a vision (or strategic direction) around which the programmes of public and private sectors could group. There are some signs of the re-emergence of long-termism: a view that the future of cities and the commitment of public and private investment in them cannot be based upon short-term pragmatism. In a number of the authorities visited in connection with the strategic planning, economic development and urban regeneration case-studies there was wide agreement that local Chambers of Commerce, CBI, and individual enterprises are pre-disposed to look to the local authority for a lead in strategic policy areas (thus reinforcing the facilitation role discussed above). The increasing emphasis upon place marketing (raising the profile of an area to encourage investment) and the re-emergence of regional guidance as the framework for structure plans reinforces the rehabilitation of planning.

As one would expect from a government much more committed to 'market' than to 'planning' approaches to the provision of local services, the service-specific planning function in local government has been diluted over the past few years, although there are some signs of a reversal of this trend at the moment. Structure planning (in relation to local authorities' land-use responsibilities) has survived, albeit in a much weakened form, in Greater London and the metropolitan conurbations (where county structure plans have been replaced by strategic guidance at county level). In general, the tendency of govern-ment to intervene in the structure planning process has increased and the presumption in favour of development which became a guiding principle of planning applications and appeals in the early 1980s is a clear illustration of the changing balance between 'the market' and 'planning' in this field.

The three major policy planning systems linking areas of local government activity with specific grant finance from central government (housing investment programmes, transportation policies and programmes, inner city programmes) have long ceased to be genuine planning documents through which (differing) local needs and priorities can be expressed and responded to. They have become, over the years, much more routinised bidding systems constrained increasingly tightly by central government policy priorities, bureaucratic monitoring and review procedures and reducing resource availability and whose time horizons have become correspondingly reduced. The latest City Challenge and Housing Investment Programme initiatives which emphasise the competitive bidding nature of planning processes reinforce the significance, but at the same time the changed culture, of planning.

In some areas of service responsibility a revived or newly imposed commitment to service planning has developed recently (waste and litter are examples). In relation to services for the elderly social service departments will be required to produce Community Care Plans for the development of services, consistent with the plans of health authorities and other interested agencies, under the 1990 National Health and Community Care Act. This change follows a decade in which social services planning statements had ceased to be required by central government.

This revival of interest in planning in relation to services for the elderly is something of a side-track by a government which has never given the planning function a high priority, but which found it hard to avoid providing local authorities with an enhanced set of responsibilities in relation to community care, following the recommendations by the Griffiths Committee. There has been little change in this direction in any of the other major service responsibility areas, and no implication that the government has re-thought the relative emphasis between markets and planning as a basis for service provision which has characterised its legislative programme since the mid 1980s. The waste disposal strategies initiated in the late 1970s have not been produced by the majority of waste disposal authorities reflecting (inter alia) the lack of pressure from central government to do so (although the DoE Inspectorate has exerted pressure in this direction). The only other service responsibility in which there has been an increase in the local authority planning function is economic development, where the 1985 Act requires an authority wishing to become involved in economic development to prepare a document setting out their proposals, and what they are intended to achieve.

What has become apparent in a number of other service

responsibility areas, however, has been the government's definition of a strategic enabling role for local authorities, partly intended to compensate for the reduction in service provision responsibility which typically accompanies it. Thus, in relation to housing where local authorities' policy and financial discretion has clearly declined markedly in recent years, a strategic enabling role is defined for local government.

In this role there will no longer be the same presumption that the local authority itself should take direct action to meet new or increasing demands. The future role of local authorities will essentially be that of identifying housing needs and demands, encouraging innovative methods of provision by other bodies to meet such needs, maximising the use of private finance and encouraging the new interest in the revival of the independent rented sector. In order to fulfil this strategic role, they will have to work closely with housing associations; private landlords; developers; and building societies and other providers of finance.

The new emphasis on a strategic enabling role (and the greater local authority discretion implied) may not be consistent with the inability of local authorities to carry out this role effectively, because of reductions in policy and financial discretion. Strategic discretion in this sense is anyway widely viewed as a problematical and largely untested power, in comparison with the more familiar powers of direct service provision.

Both strategic planning and structure planning represent areas of activity in which with a few exceptions little political discretion (or control) is exercised. They are typically officer-led exercises, with local politicians often content to rubber-stamp (or marginally amend) what officers have produced (admittedly in the light of an awareness of explicit and implicit political objectives). There is some evidence that this generality holds true for the planning function generally. It is not a function which necessarily fits easily with local politicians' familiar (and, in their terms, rational) concern for the more tangible issues of policy and policy implementation. Indeed planning is sometimes seen as unduly restrictive to future political flexibility.

Resource acquisition

In general, the British system of local government finance since 1959 can be characterised as combining a great deal of freedom both over levels of expenditure in general, and allocations between services in particular, a freedom which became constrained during the 1980s by the use of new powers to cap the local tax levels of a selected minority of local authorities. By the end of the decade the ability of local authorities to manoeuvre their way around the various attempts to restrict revenue and capital expenditure introduced by the government had been severely curtailed.

The reform of local government finance, presaged by the 1986 Green Paper 'Paying for Local Government' has undoubtedly greatly tightened the screw on local authorities on both the capital and revenue side. Even the most important residual freedom in the system, namely to finance marginal expenditure, whether revenue or capital, by a local tax has, in the event, been restricted by the threat of large-scale capping.

There has also been an increasing tendency for the government to earmark particular blocks of finance for particular purposes - the specific grant principle. This has been most noticeable in relation to the ring-fencing of the housing revenue account (which makes housing in effect a separately funded service, which cannot be subsidised from the charge-fund account), but education has also been affected by this tendency (through the formula-funding mechanism) and a specific grant is proposed for the development of services for the mentally ill. In the metropolitan county areas, one of the consequences of the abolition of the metropolitan county councils has been to separate out in these areas the budgets for police, fire and civil defence and passenger transport (all of which were precept-capped in the period 1986-89) from competition for resources from other services. The general effect of these changes has been to significantly reduce the scope for choice within local authority budgets, i.e. the allocation of resources amongst different services.

Local taxation or block grant aid are not the only sources of discretionary resources, however, and the resource acquisition function can involve the assembly of resources through at least three other routes. Firstly, fees and charges (and any remaining trading services) provide a source of income, though many of the services hitherto funded through fees and charges have been (or are potentially) subject to privatisation (for example, sports centres) or to commercialisation in some form (for example, libraries). Secondly, local authorities have access to a range of grants - general and specific - which increasingly supplement local taxation. Whilst the application by central government of the additionality principle makes a number of grant régimes less attractive to local government and reduces the incentive and discretionary capacity of authorities to compete for grant, there remain a wide range of sources of grant both within the UK and in relation to EC programmes. Indeed bidding and grantsmanship are emergent and necessary political and administrative skills at the local level. Lastly, increasing emphasis is put upon leverage and packaging as a means to the end of assembling resources for local programmes. Particularly with respect to partnership programmes and projects in physical development, in the arts, in economic development and urban regeneration, leverage is a mechanism for complementing public resources and attracting private sector commitment.

Resource allocation and distribution involve the traditional budgetary processes (with which this study is not concerned) but more significantly questions about the discretion of local authorities to allocate resources on locally decided criteria. Resource allocation involves choices about the distribution of services and resources between groups and between areas. Resource distribution raises explicitly the redistributive role of local government and the capacity of authorities to develop and implement targeted, area-based programmes and positive action and equal opportunity policies.

Organisation

A number of aspects of organisation and management process, particularly as they relate to elected members, are discussed later in this chapter. Here we take one particular element - decentralisation - because of its significance to the debate about local service planning and provision and because of its relevance to conceptions of community and locality.

Decentralisation is a particular example of the organisational form in which discretion is available to local authorities. Decentralisation is defined in broad terms as an attempt to change the relationship between those providing and those receiving services, involving the service organisation getting closer to the public and (often) also an attempt to shift the balance of power in favour of those the organisation is intended to serve. Three different sets of pressures - from an interventionist central state, from new forms of political struggle and from changed thinking about the nature of effective management - are creating in different ways the conditions for increased decentralisation. Thus some of the measures pursued by the Conservative government have sought to decentralise decision-making within council structures (for example, the insistence in the 1988 Education Reform Act on the local financial management of schools). On the other hand some of the more radical initiatives in decentralisation (Islington, Tower Hamlets) have been driven forward by local politicians, keen to develop new, more responsive, forms of council decision-making. Thirdly, many councils are experimenting with local cost and performance centres. The variety of activities described as decentralisation emphasise the point that decentralisation is not an end in itself. Rather, it should be viewed as a possible route to the achievement of strategic objectives. It is, as we noted previously, best seen as a secondary rather than a primary function of local government.

Of the three forms of decentralisation discussed above the first and third are similar in that they involve changes in management style whilst the second may involve a redistribution of political power within the authority as well as a change in management style. The kind of decentralisation in education (LMS) introduced by the Conservative government has clearly reduced local authority discretion, switching power from LEAs (and elected members) to individual schools (through their headteachers and governing bodies) and is currently the only form of decentralisation which is statutorily required (although there are numerous possibilities for extending the LMS principle into other fields of local government activity). The third form of decentralisation - cost and performance centre management - is already spreading fast within local government, and is likely to continue to do so, in that it reflects a developing consensus about the basis of good management in local authorities which have become increasingly dominated by the logic of CCT (and are increasingly suffering from resource famine). This form of decentralisation also involves a reduction in discretion on the part of the authority as a whole, and a reduction in the scope for political decision-making since the responsibility of the cost-centre manager to manage his or her budget takes a whole range of detailed decisions out of the political arena.

Schemes of decentralisation of service delivery (or access points) to the neighbourhood level have so far been much more prevalent than schemes for devolving political power or introducing local control. (Tower Hamlets represents the most advanced example of the latter.) Devolved political power, where it does occur, is almost always associated with decentralised service delivery (although there are exceptions - area planning committees for example may co-exist with a 'centralised' (in locational terms) planning department).

In terms of service responsibilities the two services which have been most emphasised in decentralisation schemes have been housing (increasingly associated with certain aspects of environmental health) and social services. In the latter case several authorities are reviewing whether patch provision (based on neighbourhoods) is compatible with the demands of the new Children Act and Community Care and Health Act. Several shire counties have decentralised their education service (often in association with local advisory committees). Multi-service neighbourhood offices are less common, although several authorities have earmarked housing decentralisation as a first phase of what they hope will in due course be a multi-service initiative.

Decentralisation in service delivery terms is perhaps most usefully seen as an alternative consumerist solution to the present government's market emphasis, i.e. as a means of improving the accessibility of services and the responsiveness of service delivery within the framework of a commitment to public provision. It is thus most likely to appeal to Labour-controlled authorities. In relation to the devolution of power to the neighbourhood level, decentralisation is best seen as a response to the limitations of the representative democracy model and/or a reflection of an awareness of the arbitrary nature of the territorial definition of many local authorities, which include (or are perceived to include) within their boundaries distinctive local communities, often with a strong sense of local identity.

Accountability and review

The final function we have identified is that of accounting for the services provided and decisions made. The concept of accountability is ambiguous and multi-faceted and the distinction must be made between political accountability (which reflects a democratic ethic and mainly takes the form of regular elections) and administrative accountability, which can take a variety of forms, of which three are of particular importance - accountability for financial probity (which reflects an economic ethic and takes the institutional form of audit), accountability for administrative propriety (which adopts a legal ethic and the form of judicial supervision) and accountability for administrative efficiency (which has come to reflect a professional ethic, and often takes the institutional form of inspection).

The concept of political accountability through electoral process is not without its problems in the modern state, particularly in a state such as Great Britain which has not in modern times been required to forge a new constitutional settlement. The formal framework of accountability in local government does not recognise the existence of party politics and as a result, the lines of responsibility and accountability are occasionally blurred. This area of uncertainty has enabled central government in recent years to de-emphasise the concept of political accountability, at the local level, and (at least partially) replace or modify it with motions of accountability to consumers of particular services (housing tenants, boards of school governors, community-charge payers).

Thus, in education, lines of accountability have been changed by the 1988 Education Reform Act in two different ways. The LEA now has a more direct line of responsibility from the DES. The relationship with the DES is top down and less two-way than in the past, with the DES assuming greater powers. In addition the LEA's relationship with schools and colleges is more indirect, with schools and colleges having increased powers of decision-making.

This two-pronged attack on local accountability - moving it upwards to the centre and downwards to individual institutions/consumers has occurred in a number of other service areas (for example, housing, where the introduction of tenants ballots over responsibility for estate management is a striking example of a switch from political accountability to market/consumer accountability).

In other service areas, accountability mechanisms, rather than changing in form, have simply become less clear. The convoluted nature of accountability processes in the joint boards which have been responsible since 1986 for police, fire and civil defence and passenger transport in the metropolitan county areas has become increasingly apparent. In the field of urban regeneration it is evident that many of the contemporary institutions of regeneration are not locally accountable. The establishment of multiple regeneration agencies on the ground has clearly diluted local accountability in two ways. First the proliferation of agencies has blurred lines of accountability with the result that there is a good deal of confusion as to who is actually responsible for what and secondly there is little local accountability in so far as many of the agencies involved have lines of accountability back to central headquarters (a function of the traditionally vertical lines of communication in central-local relationships and of the absence of corporate working at both central and local levels). In the most recent development of joint arrangements for public/private working, the emergence of 'leadership teams' raises a further point about accountability. Local leaders tend to be self-selected (or appointed) and are drawn from local influentials and from a local élite. A similar point can be made about Training and Enterprise Councils (TECs).

Indeed the past decade has seen a change in balance in the emphasis on different forms of accountability, at local level, away from the political, towards the administrative. Each of the three forms of administrative accountability has been strengthened, through the introduction of externally-imposed mechanisms. The 1989 Local Government and Housing Act, drawing upon the recommendations of the Widdicombe Report, strengthened the financial probity and administrative propriety of accountability mechanisms (at the expense of political accountability) by providing an independent legal basis for such roles within local authorities (via the specification and empowerment of the financial probity and monitoring officers respectively). The establishment in 1982 of the Audit Commission has strengthened accountability mechanisms for financial probity (local authorities losing the right to choose their auditor) and for administrative efficiency (through the Commission's duty to satisfy themselves that a local authority has made proper arrangements for the securing economy, efficiency and effectiveness in its use of resources). This change in effect challenges the professional ethic of inspection. External inspection has been limited to a selection of services and is often carried out on the basis of co-operative inter-professional relationships between inspectors and those inspected, thus depoliticising the accountability process.

The impact of functional change upon discretion and control

Having looked at changes within individual functions, it is important to examine changes in the overall pattern of local government functions over the past decade or so, and to relate these both to developments in broad service areas and to the two central concerns of the research - administrative and political discretion and control.

Service responsibilities and functional change

The social welfare services, such as education, social services and housing, are traditionally those where local government's policy discretion and redistributive capacity has been greatest. Now, it is clear that the degree of policy discretion is being constrained. Local government's ability to influence the nature and methods of service delivery and resource allocation is reduced, if not entirely eliminated. Another trend that is apparent is the tendency for the discretionary aspects of these services to be squeezed out, where statutory services compete for resources, particularly when statutory requirements are being more clearly specified by new legislation. Instead the new emphasis is on local authorities developing a strategic capacity, assessing needs, working in partnership with a diversity of other agencies and monitoring and being accountable for the quality of what is provided. This represents a marked (centrally-imposed) reduction in the direct service provision function of local government, brought about partly through the re-allocation of certain service responsibilities from local government to other agencies (UDCs, centrally-funded schools, housing associations) but mainly through the centrally-imposed switch in an increasing number of services from the direct provision function to that of service purchaser on a contract basis. This switch has in turn strengthened the local authority's regulatory function in relation to the monitoring and enforcement of contracts.

The shift to a more regulatory mode is also clear in the case of the new Social Services Inspection Units, the provisions of the Children Act, the monitoring of the national curriculum and of education provision more generally, and the regulation of the private rented sector. The potential that exists for local government to develop an enabling role (planning, purchasing, facilitating, regulating) within which local discretion can continue to be exercised, has been illustrated in relation to all of these services, but crucial factors are the level of resources and the degree of policy and financial autonomy available to local authorities.

The environmental services (waste management, environmental health, consumer protection) are undergoing substantial change due to the combined effect of new legislation and the higher public profile of environmental and consumer issues. The impact of these changes is somewhat contradictory. On the one hand, the service provision role in waste management is diminished by competition legislation, but the regulatory role is enhanced and expanded in a number of areas. This regulatory and enforcement role is increasingly specified by national or European standards and local discretion is minimal. However, there remain large areas of discretion, for example, in relation to trading standards, recycling and a range of 'green initiatives'.

The public protection services (police, fire and civil defence) are those where discretion has always been least, and arguments have been made to remove the functions from local government control or to place their financing on a national basis. There are clearly strong central influences on these services, through central control or influence over staffing and finance, and national legislation or regulations which prescribe standards and requirements. However, in relation to both police and fire our work suggests that the potential for local choice and discretion is underestimated by such arguments. There is existing variation in the nature of non-fire emergency operations, in non-crime-related police work and in preventive work in both services which depends on local conditions and demands, and there is substantial scope for expanding the commitment to prevention. Local control is an important means of facilitating this diversity and responsiveness.

There are a number of services, including economic development, leisure, arts and tourism, where local government activity has grown substantially during the 1980s, despite the financial constraints under which local government has been operating and the fact that all these services (with the exception of libraries) are entirely discretionary. Direct service provision is still important, though the local authority role is changing with the introduction of competitive tendering for management of leisure facilities. There is increasing recognition of the importance of these services as impinging on the 'quality of life' in localities, as key elements in 'place marketing' and as a major area of local innovation. Increasingly local authorities are having to look outside for the resources to expand these activities, and there are expectations again that local authorities will develop a more pro-active strategic and enabling role. The pro-active facilitation function has been taken up with increasing commitment by some authorities (sometimes predominantly in relation to economic development; sometimes on a wider basis) but not by others. In those authorities where the function has been emphasised, it has typically been viewed as a re-interpretation of the local governmental role in the face of the diminution of the direct service provision function (and in response to a more general perception of increasing centralisation). The limitations are not powers, as local government has demonstrated through its ability to develop its discretionary capacity, but the extent of financial autonomy available to spend on discretionary services.

Local authorities' commitment to the planning function has either been heavily constrained by the centrally-imposed specifications regarding plan content (TPPs, HIPs, IAPs) or has been rendered of limited value by the unpredictability of resource availability. Nonetheless, as has already been stressed, increasing numbers of authorities are placing a stronger emphasis on the (authority-wide) strategic planning function, again largely in an attempt to strengthen their governmental role in the face of what are perceived as attempts by central government to reduce it. In highways, transport and town and country planning the nature of local responsibilities has changed in a number of ways. The service provision of local authorities (bus operations, highways maintenance and construction) is substantially weaker and operated through arm's-length units or companies. Local government's planning role remains, but its capacity to fulfil this role has become fragmented and more limited by institutional reorganisation and changes in the financial régime in relation to transport. The perceived shift in the balance away from planning in favour of the market now seems to be reversing, associated with heightened concern over traffic congestion and other negative externalities associated with market-led development. However, it is not clear that local government currently has the financial resources or co-ordination powers to respond to these concerns.

Perhaps the major single observation of this whole part of our report is about the reduction in the capacity of local government to control the processes of resource acquisition and allocation. This reduction has certainly not involved a lessening of the importance of the function to the local authority, but rather a major reduction in discretion over this function brought about by the introduction of the community charge (and in particular the most recent charge-capping provisions). This change has in turn limited the scope for the voluntary exercise of the discretion to decentralise service provision on the part of local authorities (because of the costs associated with a movement in this direction), although the decentralisation of financial management has been considerably strengthened by the LMS requirements in education and by the client-contractor split implied by CCT. Decentralisation of service provision (and in some cases political power) has been viewed by some authorities as an attempt to challenge the market orientation of the government's legislative programme from an alternative philosophical starting point (in the same way that the strengthening of the pro-active facilitation function has been seen). (In the current financial climate, however, it is only the most determined of decentralists who are going ahead with their plans).

It is as if the limitations placed on local authorities' area of discretion in relation to certain of its functions (for example, direct provision, purchasing of services, service planning and resource acquisition and allocation) has either been tacitly accepted, resulting in a new type of authority with a much weaker community governance remit or has been challenged (as far as possible) through attempts to strengthen functions such as pro-active facilitation, strategic planning, decentralisation, and (in a more limited sense) the strategic enabling opportunities which appear to have been presented in services such as housing, social services and (more problematically) education. This stance implies a redefinition of (and renewed commitment to) the idea of community governance. The ability of local authorities to open up new areas of discretion in this way has, however (for all but the smaller shire districts), recently been made much more difficult by the introduction of the community charge and charge-capping.

The function that has been left in the most inconclusive state is that of accountability. External accountability requirements have certainly been extended and strengthened over the past decade, through the ombudsman role, the work of the Audit Commission especially in the field of managerial efficiency, and in the Widdicombe-related aspects of the 1989 Local Government and Housing Act which inter alia have limited and constrained the scope of local political choice. More importantly, the extension of customer choice in fields such as housing, education and passenger transport has implied a strengthening of the concept of market accountability in relation to local government services. However, it is apparent that the implications of these changes for the operation of accountability through the familiar representative democracy channels have not been addressed. The resolution of this uncertainty over competing conceptions of democracy and accountability is one of the areas most in need of clarification.

Local politics

The changes in the functional balance of local authorities discussed above have had important consequences for the role of politics in local government, and in particular for the scope for political roles, choice and control. The increase in politicisation identified by the Widdicombe Committee in 1986 and confirmed since has come face to face with the impact of a legislative programme which has implicitly (though not yet explicitly) redefined the role of politics in local government. The 1991 Internal Management Consultation paper takes the issue further. This confrontation has led to a good deal of confusion and uncertainty amongst members (and indeed officers) about the current scope for political choice and appropriate member role emphases.

The significance of the changes involved is well-illustrated by the analysis of the changes in functions. For example, the enforced withdrawal of members' formal responsibility (except where it had been delegated) for the 'direct provision' of services has involved a removal of two of the most valued areas of member activity. Although this loss of responsibility has taken place of necessity only in the range of services subject to CCT (covered by the 1980 and 1988 Acts) the principle involved - the separating out of client and contractor roles, politically and administratively - now has in many authorities a momentum which has taken it beyond the services directly affected by CCT. In addition, influential organisations such as the Audit Commission are now strongly advocating the withdrawal of members' involvement in 'detail' (for example, the administration/implementation of services; and day-to-day management issues within departments or the authority as a whole), and advising councillors to concentrate their energies on strategy, policy and performance monitoring.

The dilemma for the large number of members (probably the majority in most authorities) whose primary interest is in constituency matters (for example, local casework and local advocacy) is that the dilution of the direct service provision function reduces their main opportunities for involvement in decisions which affect their wards on a day-to-day basis, either formally (through the work of committees) or informally (through chasing up problems with those empowered to deal with them). The new emphasis on the service purchasing/contract specification function does not provide the same opportunities. Indeed one of the most striking effects of competition (and of other legislation which has reduced the direct service provision function) has been to limit the issues that may be defined as political. In particular, it was clear from our research interviews that local councillors have found it difficult to translate their concern with service delivery into the seemingly technical language of service specification and performance measurement. Although it can be argued that a potential link between such technical processes and political priorities and concerns can be made, such links have so far proved very difficult to realise in most authorities.

Even the policy-making role which members are being exhorted to concentrate upon is widely perceived as much more limited in scope than it used to be for two reasons: limited resource availability (see above) and the narrowing of policy choice in many of the key areas concerned (for example, housing and education).

As we have argued, the function of strategic planning, although espoused (sometimes somewhat superficially) in increasing numbers of local authorities, has proved difficult for the majority of members to grasp and relate to their political priorities. Suspicion of the change in this direction is not uncommon, coupled with the feeling that the political role is being marginalised. Strategy formulation is typically officer-led, with at best a small number of members playing a pro-active role.

There is little enhanced scope for members either in the regulatory role which (we have argued) is increasing in relative significance in local government's range of functions. Although in many authorities members do get involved in certain kinds of regulatory activities (licensing, planning control), in general this function does not provide much scope for political choice. Nor has the board member role emphasised in general terms by the Audit Commission and realised more specifically in the DSO management boards which have been set up in several authorities yet appeared to have much appeal for elected members. The decentralisation function does offer a good deal of scope for emphasising and channelling members' constituency role interests, but, as we have seen, the further development of this function in local government has been at best temporarily checked by lack of resources.

In summary, members are being faced with a bewildering and (to them) inconsistent set of pressures to modify their role patterns. There is a widespread feeling that the traditional processes of local political accountability have been diminished, without it yet being clear what has replaced them.

Discretion and control - preliminary conclusions

The main conclusions about discretion and control which emerge from the above discussion are:

(i) the past decade has seen a marked decrease in the discretion available to local authorities in relation to:

- the scope and content of local policies and service provision (especially in education, housing and the social welfare services)
- the level and allocation of locally determined resources as well as centrally determined grant
- the mode of service provision especially in respect of education, social services, waste disposal and services subject to CCT.

(ii) This marked decrease in local discretion (and conversely the increase in central control) has not taken place uniformly across service areas and there are a number of areas where both powers and duties have increased - economic development, food and litter for example). Nevertheless, the overall impact of change is unambiguous in that the United Kingdom now has a more centralised local government system than it had twenty years ago.

(iii) The most fundamental change in the pattern of local

discretion has come through the impact of the 'provider to purchaser' shift. The momentum of this shift has increased and now affects all service areas including a number not explicitly subject to CCT or purchasing requirements.

(iv) At the same time the functions of 'facilitation' and 'regulation' - which with 'purchasing' are often bundled together into a single 'enabling' have emerged as key local authority functions. Each has a different implication for local discretion. Regulation involves relatively little local discretion other than (some administrative discretion) whereas facilitation is a more pro-active function with considerable discretionary scope.

(v) There is evidence of a higher profile strategic and service planning function, in part discretionary in response to a widely felt need for longer term direction, in part mandatory in response to the need to set a framework for market activities and make (competitive) bids for resources. The resource acquisition and allocation function has been subject to severe reductions in local discretion.

(vi) Local discretion to establish organisational structures and processes has been constrained in some major respects (for example, in respect of relations with schools and in the management of CCT) but discretion has remained to establish centralised or decentralised structures of consultation, decision making, or delivery. Many authorities have felt it appropriate to carry out structural reorganisation to cope with the cumulative pressure of legislative change and loss of discretionary power.

(vii) whilst there has been a proliferation of review and accounting procedures and the emergence of wider inspectorial and regulatory functions, local democratic accountability to consumers, clients and users on the one hand and elected members on the other has not become noticeably greater. Administrative and financial accountability are being substituted for political accountability.

(viii) switches in the emphasis of local government functions have posed problems and dilemmas for local politicians in that traditional roles of local policy-making and control of service delivery have been diluted whilst the nature of the political input into newer strategic planning or regulatory functions remains as yet unclear.

(ix) there are increasing difficulties in pursuing policies which necessarily involve action across the local authorities' activities, rather than involving just one service or another.

(x) the concept of the enabling authority inhibits consideration of the institution of local government as a territorial distribution of authority which goes beyond the services that it delivers.

CHAPTER 2

THE ROLE OF LOCAL GOVERNMENT

Introduction

At the outset we noted the high level of uncertainty and instability within the current world of local government. The source of this instability and uncertainty is in part a consequence of different ideological positions about the basic purposes of local government and in part a dispute about the way such purposes should be realised - the role of local government about which there are differences both between and within major political parties.

The preceding analysis of function suggested that the very simple distinction between 'enabler' and 'provider' does not capture the functional discretion which still remains open to local government despite the limitations set upon local autonomy. The next task of this report is to offer an analytic framework within which alternative models of role and function can be appraised. There are four reasons to justify such a framework.

(i) discussion of local government futures is dominated by considerations - often short term - of finance. Though financial solutions should follow from rather than precede consideration of role, function and structure in practice the latter are often given scant attention.

(ii) there is continuing loose thinking about local government role and function, with the emergence of over-simple conceptions of what the appropriate role might be. In recent years both the enabling council and community government are open to this charge of over-simplification. Failure to clarify what is implied can lead to a failure in the organisational design of reformed systems.

(iii) this failure in design seems likely to lead to the incorporation of conflicting goals, incompatible tasks and inconsistent structures into a reconstructed local government. It is essential at this time not to build inevitable failure into the outcome of the current review of role and function.

(iv) despite the widely held stereotype of a local government system wasting away to premature demise there is a real danger of overload. Overload in the 1990s (in contrast to the 1960s and 1970s) would be the consequence of a shrinking resource base, the redefinition of functions in traditional service areas, the acquisition of mandatory and discretionary responsibilities on a number of new fronts, and the deepening of range of accountability requirements.

Our approach has been to identify a limited number of ideal types of local government. The use of ideal types is a well-established device for clarifying the key choices involved in a situation in which there exists a variety of competing ideas about the basis of structuring an activity. The key argument is that there is no single ideal system of local government which can be recommended as a thing in itself; the appropriate qualities of the system depend on the nature of the purposes and role envisaged for it.

The ideal types which are discussed below are first a reflection of the analysis of changing functions as revealed by current and evolving policy and practice (and as discussed in Chapter 1 above). Secondly, however, the analysis of role draws upon a restatement of some of the basic justifications of local government which stem from a range of theoretical, philosophical and ideological considerations. Some people may argue that the changes of recent years have rendered discussion of the basics of local government irrelevant or unnecessary. We reject this view. Too much of the 'ad-hoccery' of the last quarter of a century has failed to be grounded in basic statements about the purpose and role of local government. It is not suggested that all the justifications set out below are compatible or indeed acceptable. We do consider, however, that it is important to restate and reformulate these justifications - however briefly - so that the current debate may recognise the importance of and be informed by principle rather than pragmatism.

The justifications for local government
Political and legal justifications

The role of local government as a political institution is justified by four principles. First, local government represents the form in which some diffusion of power is assured in an essentially unitary state. Secondly, local government represents the base for political participation without which any form of politics, and representative democracy in particular, withers. Local government is the vehicle for the participation of people first as voters and secondly as elected councillors. Thirdly, local government has an educational role (as the breeding ground for MPs but also more importantly as the arena within which the art of politics is learned). Lastly local government has greater capacity to identify local needs, greater responsiveness to those needs and greater sensitivity to local political demands.

The essence of this argument is that politics is central to the proper functioning of local government and that political choice and political decision-making lie at the heart of the rationale for having a local government system at all. It is less common to see legal considerations included in a discussion of the ideological and philosophical basis of local government but the legal position is increasingly crucial with three themes being central. First is the question of accountability and the different formal forms of financial, administrative and political accountability. Secondly come questions of accountability and about standard-setting, regulation, enforcement and inspection. The principles which underlie the extent to which such procedures are legally defined or are left to political or administrative discretion are crucial in determining the autonomy or dependency of local government. Lastly comes the issue of reliance upon specific statute for the powers vested in local government, of the consequent importance of ultra vires, and of the absence of a general power of competence.

Economic justifications

In considering the economic justifications for the role of government the distinction is typically made between stabilisation, allocation and distributive roles. The traditional view has been that the local government role should be predominantly confined to the allocative function with stabilisation and distribution left to the centre. The last two decades, however, show evidence of a challenge to this presumption and much of the conflict of the 1980s has been over the extent to which local government has or should have influence over stabilisation and/or distribution as well as allocation in the local economy.

The allocative role of local government stems both from ideologies which hold that market mechanisms are inherently inappropriate for some of the goods and services which must be provided at the local level, and from a pragmatism which observes both that markets fail in certain circumstances and that the market is inefficient with respect to certain types of good. Market failure emerges where externalities arise, where information is imperfect, where there are barriers to entry into the market for potential consumers or producers, and where there are public or merit goods (extreme cases of externalities). Historically local government has had mandatory and discretionary responsibility for the management of market failure in a number of ways - through the control of externalities (public and environmental health, traffic management, amenity open space), through the management of merit and public goods (street lighting, town planning, education), through the provision of information (trading standards, advice and information services), and through direct provision where the costs of entry might exclude private provision and there is an additional public good argument (fire, police, waste). Local authorities, however, have also contributed to market failure in so far as they have established effective municipal monopolies for individual services and have allocated resources according to bureaucratic and professional criteria rather than market criteria.

Socio-geographic justifications

The key defining characteristic of local government is its localness, expressed in part by political attributes relating to participation and local choice and in part by economic attributes relating to local public goods. Ideas of locality and community have seen a significant revival in the last five years and there has been much discussion of the attributes of community government. We suggest that the proper application of the community government idea should emphasise the plurality of communities (of both place and interest) and the role of local government as a mediator of community competition and conflict rather than as the expression of a single community identity. At the same time the most recent research on locality fails to reveal any unifying characteristics upon which a system of local government might be designed. Existing local authority boundaries are as likely to hinder as assist the formation of communities and by splitting localities or artificially combining them may dilute such community as exists.

An alternative route to the identification of appropriate areas upon which to base geographical division of power lies in the identification of functional areas. These are reflections of patterns of social and economic activity - travel to work, shopping, leisure, use of public services such as health, library and further education - and are often expressed in terms of catchment areas for local service use or shopping, of local labour markets, or of local media coverage.

Towards a typology of local government roles

Different ideological and philosophical starting points produce different interpretations of what the role and function of a local government system should be in practice. There are, however, two key dimensions upon which the identification of ideal types (or models) can be based.

These dimensions stem explicitly from two of the justifications for local government discussed above, and are reflected first in a political dimension, the balance between central and local responsibility for the government of local communities and secondly an economic dimension, the balance between the role of the markets and the role of public provision of goods in local service provision.

The political dimension

The first key dimension is that which distinguishes between a weak role for local government (in the sense of a narrow range of functional responsibilities, a reactive mode of operation, a low level of autonomy/discretion within those functions, and a high degree of external control), and a strong role (implying a wider range of functions, pro-active range of operation, high levels of autonomy/discretion and more limited levels of external control). This is a dimension which responds explicitly to the central theme of this research, namely the availability or absence of local discretion and control administrative or political control.

The economic dimension

In the Conservative government's post-1987 legislative programme there has been an increasing emphasis on the role of the market in local government, both as an alternative source of provision of services, and as a set of conditions which should be replicated as far as possible for the provision of services which it is accepted should remain within the public sector (the concept of quasi-markets). Thus a key dimension of the current debate is the choice between high market emphasis in the production and distribution of local goods and services and a high emphasis on public sector agencies in the production and distribution of local goods and services.

The interplay of these two dimensions is depicted in Diagram 3. The implication is that a strong market emphasis can co-exist in principle with either a weak or a strong role for local government, and that similarly, a strong public sector emphasis can co-exist with either a weak or strong local government role. Taking in each case the extreme positions, there are four potential variants: strong market/weak local government; strong public sector/weak local government; strong market/strong local government; and strong public-sector/strong local government. There are of course a number of intermediate positions which could also be identified on the diagram reflecting (for example) mixed economy or central-local partnership ideologies.

There is, however, a third socio-geographic dimension which must be conceptually superimposed upon the diagram reflecting the socio-geographic justifications for local government discussed above. This dimension reintroduces the concepts of locality, territoriality and scale into the analysis recognising the difference between a local government which is characterised by local identity, a community orientation, small scale and active participation on the one hand and large scale, bureaucratic and unresponsive organisation and a representational political form on the other. Though not represented on Diagram 3 this dimension is discussed again later.

DIAGRAM 3 - A Framework for Analysis.

Weak Local Government Role
Restricted range of Responsibilities
Low Autonomy

Strong Market
Strong Private Control

Weak Market
Strong Public Control

Strong Local Government Role
Wide range of Responsibilities
High Autonomy

Ideal types in theory

In order to show how this framework of analysis is relevant to our earlier discussion of service responsibilities and functions, we have identified a number of ideal types each of which incorporates a different conception of the key dimensions of the framework. Each ideal type reflects in a particular way some of the characteristics of a local government system (territorial structure, resource acquisition and use, political management structure, forms of accountability and so on). These seven ideal types, illustrated in Diagram 4 overleaf, have been labelled:

(i)   the residual authority
(ii) the administrative agent
(iii) the traditional bureaucratic authority
(iv) the self-sufficient authority
(v) the market-oriented enabler

(vi) the regulatory authority
(vii) the community oriented enabler

DIAGRAM 4
Ideal Types for the Analysis of Local Government

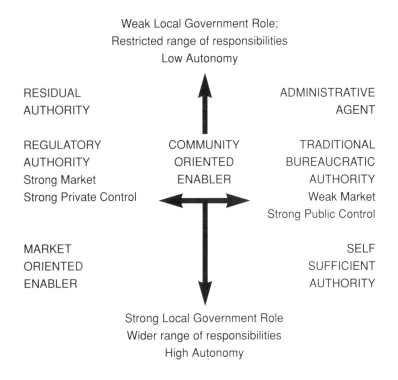

Weak Local Government Role;
Restricted range of responsibilities
Low Autonomy

RESIDUAL
AUTHORITY

ADMINISTRATIVE
AGENT

REGULATORY
AUTHORITY
Strong Market
Strong Private Control

COMMUNITY
ORIENTED
ENABLER

TRADITIONAL
BUREAUCRATIC
AUTHORITY
Weak Market
Strong Public Control

MARKET
ORIENTED
ENABLER

SELF
SUFFICIENT
AUTHORITY

Strong Local Government Role
Wider range of responsibilities
High Autonomy

The residual authority

The term residual (or minimalist) refers to the emphasis placed in this ideal type upon the local authority as a provider of last resort, responsible only for a limited set of services which cannot be provided directly through the private market or through some other more appropriate mechanism (for example, quango, development corporation, local office of central government). Even in the case of those residual services for which a local authority would retain responsibility, it would not be expected that the responsibility would be exercised directly. Rather the

46

authority would be expected to specify the level of service required, contract out the service to a private contractor (or exceptionally a local authority in-house contracting agency) and then to monitor the contractor's performance. There would also be some regulation of private sector activity, but even this role would be minimised, because from this ideological stand-point, the market can be trusted as the most efficient and effective mechanism for providing goods and services of all kinds, with only few exceptions and with only a limited need for regulation.

The key accountability relationship would be between the individual community charge-payer and the local authority, the transaction being viewed as involving as close an approximation as possible to a market transaction between customer and market organisation. Notions of community (in terms of a wider social network or territorial identity) are not seen as significant. The idea that a local authority should play any wider role in terms of defining and meeting local community needs would in consequence be seen as inappropriate. (The local authority merely enables the provision of a limited range of public goods and services, which the market cannot provide.)

The administrative agent

This ideal type is premised on a much stronger perception of the inappropriateness of the market as a mechanism for the provision and distribution of a wide range of public goods and services, particularly in view of the perceived inequality of access to such goods and services amongst different income groups when such services are provided on a market basis. However, standards of provision are viewed as best decided at a national level where, in particular, major decisions on the redistribution of resources and benefits would take place. The key role of the administrative agent authority would be to administer and co-ordinate a wide range of public services, with a limited degree of discretion to vary service levels to reflect differences in local circumstances. The key financial linkages between centre and locality would reflect a system of specific grants (based on some kind of bidding system) supplemented only by a general needs-related central government grant, with limited scope to raise resources locally. There would be a strong regulatory role for the centre in relation to the functional responsibilities of local authorities, and a strong external mechanism for grievance redress. Service provision guidelines (or quality control) would be specified by the centre.

The traditional bureaucratic authority

Although local government as an institution has been moving away from the ideal of the self-sufficient authority it would be unrealistic to characterise the archetypal local authority of the 1945-76 period as self-sufficient. The implied level of discretion of such self-sufficiency in terms of finance, policy and general powers, did not exist in this period. There is a much stronger emphasis in the traditional bureaucratic authority on service delivery and on the local council as controller of a set of discrete services rather than a vehicle of community government. Statutory duties are seen as the main justification for the council's activities; professional disciplines form the basis of departmental and committee organisation. Public needs are interpreted by professionals who view recipients as reactive clients. This type of authority does not spend much time looking outwards for opportunities to identify public needs and meet them. There is strong emphasis upon public provision as opposed to the market and an expectation though not necessarily the utilisation of a high level of discretion. Representative democracy (through service committees and service committee representation on Policy and Resources) is the main form of accountability.

The self-sufficient authority

This position has traditionally represented the preferred option of most local authorities in Britain, although it is questionable how close to the ideal type the reality ever approached, even in the relatively conflict-free partnership-emphasising years prior to 1979. Accepting that the degree of autonomy from central government on the part of local government can never be total (except in a federal system, for specified areas of responsibility) the self-sufficient authority offers a combination of the maximum acceptable degree of local authority autonomy with a maximum emphasis on the public sector as the key agency in the production and distribution of local goods and services. In conjunction with this ideal type, therefore, there would be no requirement nor expectation that a local authority should use outside contractors to provide services unless it chose to. The main mechanisms for identifying and responding to need would thus be internal and dominated as traditionally by professional/departmental interests working to professionally-defined client needs, under the direction of a political system premised upon strong representative democracy.

There would be scope (not necessarily realised in practice) for an overview of community needs which went beyond the specific functional responsibilities which the authority had been given, and the development of a plan of action to respond to them. Indeed this ideal type is congruent with a general competence power and a strong and buoyant source of local taxation to fulfil the logic of its requirements.

The market-oriented enabler

This ideal type emphasises (in common with the residual authority) the primacy of the market in the affairs of the local authority, but from a very different starting point. The philosophy of the market-oriented enabler places the local authority in a much stronger and more pro-active role in relation to the economic future of its area and the provision of services than does that of the residual authority. The local authority is seen as the key planning and co-ordinating agency for local economic development, providing a series of mechanisms and incentives through which the local economy can flourish. The planning role of the authority is given much more emphasis, embodying a view that a longer-term planned approach to land-use, infrastructure, transportation and public services is necessary for the effective operation of the local economy. The relation between the local authority and local economic concerns is seen as a two-way process. Social responsibility on the part of the local employer is emphasised and planning agreements between developer and local authority expected and pro-actively negotiated. The concepts of leverage and pump-priming are emphasised in the local authority's approach to the encouragement and support of private enterprise.

Although the market (as contractor) would again normally be relied upon in relation to consumption services, the approach would be different from that of the residual authority. Attempts would be made to negotiate contracts which maximised the benefits to the local authority, rather than the adoption of the more passive least-cost contract-letting mechanism for a limited number of specified services emphasised by the residual authority. There would be more recognition of the need to regulate the activities of the private sector, premised on a lesser degree of implicit trust in the ability of the market to deliver (or at least to do so without undesirable externalities). The importance of the local authority as a focal point in a network of external (primarily private sector) linkages would be emphasised.

The regulatory authority

An ideal type of the future (as opposed to the past) is the regulatory authority. This has a strong market emphasis but a view of the market and its operation which acknowledges the need for a publicly accountable body to play a strong regulatory role. This ideal type is comparable in a number of ways with the residual type but gives much more emphasis in relation to privatisation, contracting-out and quasi-markets to the need for public regulation. The regulatory model draws its principles from the theories of public goods and market failure discussed earlier. The regulatory authority might retain some direct service provision responsibilities but its primary role would be to regulate the activities of others in the interests of the welfare of residents. It is predicated upon modest local discretion and reliance upon national standards and formal procedures for assessment and review. Regulation is dominated by professional and inspectorial staff who rely on a strong centre for support in their inspection and enforcement functions. The regulatory authority is largely apolitical and elected members are respected for their technical rather than their political skills.

The use of this ideal typology lies in its potential for clarifying the differing conceptions of a local authority. Nevertheless these first six types fail in certain respects. Most importantly they omit any consideration of the locality basis upon which government might be based and therefore do not reflect characteristics of the area basis of function, community or locality. The most fundamental justifications for local government lie in socio-geographic considerations relating to community and area (see page 42 above). It is extremely hard to fit area based conceptions of local government into the ideal type framework of Diagrams 3 and 4 since the six main extreme cases do not have particular or exclusive locality connotations. To incorporate spatial thinking, however, a further ideal type has been located at the centre of the diagrams.

The community-oriented enabler

This type rests upon the argument that even in the apparently restrictive context of local authority operations caused by the post-1987 legislative programme, there remains an alternative interpretation of the enabling authority role. This ideal type (which is between the market enabler and self-sufficiency positions) is premised on the view that a local authority should exist to meet the varied needs of its resident, working and visitor population, using whatever channels of provision (local authority direct provision, private sector, voluntary sector) and influence seem most appropriate.

There is an emphasis on collective as well as individual needs, and especially on the idea of communities. There is an emphasis on the role of the local authority resident as citizen which goes beyond the implications of consumer/customer roles. This ideal type implies a heightened emphasis on participatory democracy (although not necessarily as an alternative to representative democracy) and community accountability (as opposed to accountability to the market or to the wider political party). It implies an outward-looking networking role through which influence can be exerted. It is the alternative within which decentralised forms of local government most logically fit. As with any ideal type, the community-oriented enabling role would be subject to the constraints of whatever national policies or standards were in operation in relation to its range of activities, but it would operate in conjunction with significant local autonomy.

Ideal types in practice

How useful are these ideal types in understanding the contemporary position and behaviour of local authorities? The first picture which emerges strongly from our research is of a local government system which is being dragged away from its familiar traditional role by the weight and nature of legislative change since 1987. But it is being propelled not towards the local authority's own preferred option (self-sufficiency) but rather away from that option. For local government the choice is between the residual, market enabler and community enabler roles. Some authorities are extremely reluctant to face that choice and are striving to retain an identity based on the direct service emphasis of the traditional bureaucratic role (this category including a surprisingly large number of Conservative-controlled authorities).

The increasing numbers of authorities that have faced up to the choice have moved - sometimes explicitly, sometimes implicitly - either in the direction of the residual authority - Rochford, Wansdyke, Wandsworth, for example - or in the direction of a position somewhere between the community enabler and market enabler roles. In some cases the former emphasis has been apparent (Tower Hamlets, Islington, Rochdale), in others, the latter (Trafford, Bradford (in the late 1980s), Arun). The basis of the emphasis is partly political - Conservative-controlled authorities rarely emphasise the community enabler role - and partly circumstantial - some authorities have more urgent and pressing problems of economic decline/regeneration than others.

The choice is also circumscribed in that central government has been clearly supportive of a move towards the residual role, agnostic about a move in the direction of the market enabler role (there is support of the right of local authorities to play this role but with new financial and operational restrictions) and not at all supportive of the move towards the community enabler role (which the increasing financial restrictions have made more difficult, not to mention the constraints on the mode of service delivery built in to many of the major pieces of legislation).

Nevertheless, it is clear that a surprisingly high proportion of authorities have taken a pro-active rather than a re-active view of enabling, on a whole range of criteria from collection of information about community needs, increased interaction with the private sector, to a greater propensity to develop authority-wide strategies. Thus when faced with the choice, they have tried to move into the bottom left-hand quadrant of Diagram 3/4 rather than the top left-hand quadrant. They have tried to emphasise the governmental (rather than service administration) aspects of their operations, recognising that this role has increasingly to be realised through external influence rather than direct power.

In particular service areas these choice processes are also apparent. The Education case-study identifies three ideal types particular to education.

> LEAs within this study had very different values, ideologies and political purposes. Their approaches to the delivery of their education services can be broadly categorised as enabling or traditional ... a common political assumption behind the enabling perspective is that education has to be transformed, and principles of party instilled into all educational activities ... the traditional perspective is based on assumptions about 'one nation' and the value of education as a public good.
>
> Two very different models of enabling LEAs emerge. The first can be described as the enabling LEA with egalitarian or redistributive purpose ... the second as the enabling LEA as a corporate business. The objectives of the former are rooted in core values of equality or opportunity ... such authorities adopt intervention as a political strategy in the belief that education is a dynamic process which can contribute towards the transformation of society. This approach to intervention emphasises the importance of the local authority, as opposed to central government, as the vehicle through which locally responsive education is provided.
>
> The LEA as a corporate business operates as corporate company with the political leadership acting as directors of holding companies. Such an LEA is likely to be constitutionalist, drawing heavily on the legal framework which it sees as determining the scope and nature of the local

authority services which it provides. Its financial and its educational planning framework reflects its corporate business orientation. It has a regular financial planning cycle.

The traditional LEA argues that a supportive and relatively non-interventionist approach by the central administration to schools and colleges contributes to the improvement of the quality of teaching.

This shows that, even though the exercise of discretion within the field of education is decreasing, there are still real choices of role emphasis to be made. Similarly in housing, interpretation of the new nominally strategic housing role specified for local authorities by central government varies considerably, with some authorities emphasising (and trying to accelerate) the residual nature of their housing functions, whilst others have been concerned to emphasise a more pro-active enablement stance (with a strong tendency in this particular field towards community enablement, especially in the area office/committee systems developed in authorities like Walsall, Bristol and Rochdale).

Evidence on grant aid demonstrates that whilst some authorities are trying to restructure their relationship with the voluntary sector on a contract basis (resources provided for services rendered), reflecting a move towards the residual role, others are trying to maintain a relationship which reflects a much stronger commitment to voluntary groups as a key element in the authority's view of its role (reflecting a move in the community enabler direction). In economic development there is a range of approaches, some involving a wide-ranging and imaginative set of initiatives, and others a much more low key re-active approach. Similar conclusions arise from the urban regeneration case-study which illustrates the variety of pro-active local authority led approaches to town and city futures.

As noted in Section 2, there is widespread scepticism about the feasibility of many of the service-specific strategic roles identified by the government - services for the elderly and housing for example - in the light of the mismatch between the demands of a strategic role and the finance available. However, this has not prevented local authorities exploiting strategic and enabling opportunities where they have been able to, just as (until recently) they have been able to generate more financial discretion than the government intended. So far, however, the choice process has been a largely re-active one, unstructured by any clear picture of central government's own view of local government key purposes and rules. It is time that view was made explicit, and the implication more systematically explored.

Diagram 5 overleaf summarises the key features of the seven ideal types providing the basis for an assessment and evaluation of their respective relevance and merits. The Diagram attempts to capture in simple form the key features of each 'ideal type'. It points to the primary role, main functions, scope for discretion together with other key features. The main evaluation of different models and their implications for immediate policy issues emerge, however, in Chapter 3.

DIAGRAM 5
Key Features of the Seven Ideal Types

	Primary Role	Main Functions
RESIDUAL AUTHORITY	Provider of Last Resort Filler of "Market Gaps" Weak PLC Role	Contract specification and monitoring Limited regulation
ADMINISTRATIVE AGENT	Administration/ implementation of nationally-determined service	Service provision Regulation Co-ordination
TRADITIONAL BUREAUCRATIC	Direct responsibility for a wide range of services	Service Provision Co-ordination External advocacy
SELF-SUFFICIENT AUTHORITY	Direct responsibility for provision of wide range of local services	Service provision Strategic Advocacy Redistributory
MARKET-ORIENTED ENABLER	Key agency for local economic development. Strong PLC role	Contract specification and monitoring Advocacy Bargaining
REGULATORY AUTHORITY	Regulation of contractors providing services for local authority and of private sector activities	Contract specification and monitoring Wide scope of regulatory and inspectorial activity
COMMUNITY ORIENTED-ENABLING	Comprehensive identification of community needs, and responsibility (not necessarily direct) for meeting them	Mixed mode of service provision Strategic; Advocacy Redistributory

Scope for Discretion	Other Key Features
Low	Contract-dominated consumer emphasis Clear client/contractor split Market accountability Emphasis on 'charging'
Low (except for administrative discretion)	Rule-dominated Limited scope for political control Bureaucratic mode of service delivery
Moderate	Emphasis on statutory duties Professional/client emphasis in services Representative democracy
High	Professional/client emphasis in services Representative democracy and accountability processes Strong political control
High (Policy content) Low (mode of service delivery)	Contract-dominated Local business emphasis Clear client/contractor split Corporate accountability
Low	Emphasis on European/national standards Limited scope for political control Emphasis on client contractor split
High	Community-emphasis Participative decision-making Area/neighbourhood orientation Community accountability

CHAPTER 3

FUTURE DIRECTIONS

Introduction

In this final chapter, the main aim is to draw out the implications of the findings set out in Chapter 1 of this report, and the analysis contained in Chapter 2, for the current debate about the future of local government. We argued in the introduction that local government as an institution was currently at a crossroads. There has been a major change of direction implicit in the programmes of all parties away from the traditional bureaucratic authority, with its pretensions to self-sufficiency. Where it is a movement to is by no means yet clear, however.

The implications of this uncertainty about future direction are that there is also no clarity over the appropriateness of any of the many more specific ideas currently in circulation about aspects of finance, political role, or local government structure (territorial or organisational). Thus elected mayors, unitary authorities, decentralisation, the council tax, strategic planning - can only logically be evaluated if and when there is greater clarity about the fundamental purpose and role of local government. Some of the links between primary roles and the more specific features of local government which were briefly examined in Chapter 2 are discussed in more detail in this concluding section. The approach adopted is to draw out - first in tabular form, and then through a more extended analysis - the implications of each ideal type for five key attributes of a local government system: finance, political roles and management structures, internal structures and processes, territorial structure (including local authority size), and accountability processes.

At the outset it is important to make the general point that almost all the possible features of a (reformed) local government system which have been advocated by proponents of change from all political parties (and ideological positions within them) can be demonstrated to exist and to operate if not successfully, then with no palpably demonstrable adverse consequences, in some other European or Western countries (the community charge constitutes an exception). An advocate for almost any feature of local government can invariably find a successful example of what he or she is advocating. For example, advocates of directly-elected city mayors can point to West Germany and the USA; regional government is strong in Spain and Italy (indeed several European countries have a federal system in which legislative and revenue-raising powers are delegated to sub-national governmental bodies). Voting systems based on proportional representation (of which there are several varieties) are now the norm in Western Europe. In Scandinavia there is now a 'free local government' experiment in operation, whereby some local government units, on application, may be exempted from existing legislation (if they feel it hampers their ability to respond to local circumstances) and are permitted to determine their own alternative bye-laws, subject to ministerial approval. Authorities of much smaller size than 50,000 are common in Sweden, Norway and France (amongst other countries) where joint action is correspondingly common and largely unproblematical. Most European countries operate multi-tier systems of sub-national government without experiencing or perceiving the problems associated with such systems which are emphasised by advocates of unitary authorities in England.

Similarly there are widely varying arrangements for service provision with local provision being the responsibility of the central State, regional or local governments, the private sector, mixed organisations or non-statutory or voluntary organisations. The obsession with service responsibilities - planning, provision or delivery - is a peculiarly ethno-centric British concern deriving from the specific historical tradition of local government in the UK.

Differences in practice between countries are typically explained by reference to the different historical traditions, cultural environments, and political dynamics of the countries concerned. Nonetheless the general implication of the existence of the variety of system components and modes of operation outlined above is an important one. There is little, if anything, on the current agenda of change for which working parallels somewhere in Europe or elsewhere cannot be identified. Four clear trends emerge, however:

(i) in other European countries there is broad movement towards decentralisation rather than the reverse;

(ii) in most other countries service considerations are a weaker explanation of or justification for local government than in the UK;

(iii) whilst there is evidence of the successful, existence of small authorities in other countries in most cases community government co-exists with a wider, often regional tier (analogous to local - parish - councils and local authorities in England);

(iv) the merits of variety are widely recognised and there is potential for the co-existence of small and large authorities within a local government system.

In practice there is sufficient variety of arrangements with regard to local government in the four countries comprising the United Kingdom to make the point about diversity without moving across the English Channel. Northern Ireland stands out as perhaps the most centralised system of local government in Europe with local municipalities holding only an extremely limited range of powers. In Great Britain, there is a country wide two-tier system of government in Scotland (with the exception of the Island authorities) with a regional tier carrying responsibilities in the urban areas as well as in rural areas. The legal basis for a number of services differs in Scotland as do arrangements for financial control (the Accounts Commission rather than the Audit Commission). In England the two-tier system operates only in the shire counties, metropolitan local government being concentrated since 1974 in districts (or in London in the Boroughs). Welsh local government whilst currently operating on the two-tier basis does so with different service responsibilities at county and district level than in England.

Northern Ireland illustrates well the residual model discussed earlier in this report, though there is evidence of local councils becoming involved with new services such as leisure and recreation. A most striking feature of the Northern Ireland experience, however, is the role of the elected member in a residual system. Denied power over services, and dominated by central interests in the Boards (of Education and Libraries, for example) councillors concentrate heavily on issues of local electoral salience. This may be due to the electoral system itself (proportional representation) but suggests that a residual model offers little incentive to the councillor to become involved in strategic issues. Indeed the absence of a strategic role forces elected members into the parochial model.

The most significant variation, however, is widely felt to be the different relationships between central and local government in Scotland and Wales as opposed to England. The cosy relationship with a single Minister and with an integrated Scottish/Welsh Office is well documented and is widely thought to be a model which explains not only a a more robust local government in these two countries but also a greater degree of local variation and discretion at the local level. Certainly the close relationship with the Scottish and Welsh Offices sustains a better understanding of local problems and allows a more flexible approach. In Scotland the existence of a single Local Authority Association also helps to sustain a close central-local link.

It is also possible, however, to recognise the Scottish and Welsh systems as ones of central co-option rather than relative local autonomy. Certainly central government in Scotland and Wales exercises more control over service planning and delivery than do English departments or regional offices. It is appropriate to contrast the alleged merits of a single Secretary of State and an integrated civil service in Scotland and Wales with the same structure in Northern Ireland. The net observation from this research, therefore, is that whilst the institutional arrangements differ significantly within the UK and whilst working practices are consequently much easier and more efficient in Scotland and Wales, the extent of central control and conversely the degree of local discretion do not vary as much as the apparent close central-local relationship might suggest. The analysis of role and function that we offer is appropriate throughout the UK.

DIAGRAM 6

THE IMPLICATIONS OF THE SEVEN IDEAL TYPES FOR STRUCTURES AND PROCESSES

Characteristics of Process and Structure	THE RESIDUAL AUTHORITY
Financial implications	
(i) Basic source of revenue	Charging (emphasising community charge)
(ii) Subsidiary sources of revenue	Limited needs-equalisation top-up of central grant
Political implications	
(i) Political management structures	Small management board meeting 2/3 a year
(ii) Key political roles	Board member Contract legitimation
Organisational implications	
(i) Scope for authority-wide strategic planning	Inappropriate
(ii) Basis of service provision and planning	Market-led service provision - customer preference the key influence
(iii) Basis of internal organisation	Contract specification and management Small authority - 'all centre'
(iv) Approach to external relationships	Unnecessary (except with contractors)
Implications for Territorial structure	Small (c 50,000) 'all purpose' authorities plus quangos, joint action and switch of functions to the centre
Implications for Accountability and Control	
(i) Main accountability link	Via the chargepayer/consumer
(ii) Basis of control and inspection	Market signals

THE REGULATORY AUTHORITY

Charging (emphasising community charge)
More extensive level of central grant
(c.f. residual authority)

Small council or management board meeting irregularly
Board member
Performance monitor

Inappropriate

Market-led customer preference, professional
expertise
Contract-specification and management plus
(multi-purpose) inspectorate
Limited (some contact with producer interests)

Small (c 50, 000 authorities if regulation 'contracted out'
Otherwise larger units based on economies of scale

Professional standards legal sanctions
Market signals, legislation

DIAGRAM 6 (continued)

Characteristics of Process and Structure	THE ADMINISTRATIVE AGENT
Financial implications	
(i) Basic source of revenue	Central and specific grants
(ii) Subsidiary sources of revenue	Limited source of local revenue
Political implications	
(i) Political management structures	Service (administration) committees
(ii) Key political roles	Local representative casework
Organisational implications	
(i) Scope for authority-wide strategic planning	Very limited - mainly co-ordinating
(ii) Basis of service provision and planning	Functional/bureaucratic administration central guidelines
(iii) Basis of internal organisation	Service departments Co-ordinating central role
(iv) Approach to external relationships	Limited, (except to central govt.)
Implications for Territorial structure	Based on economics of production/ distribution; Multi-tier system likely functions to the centre
Implications for Accountability and Control	
(i) Main accountability link	To individual citizen via external regulation appeal
(ii) Basis of control and inspection	National inspectorates/ appeal mechanisms

THE TRADITIONAL BUREAUCRATIC AUTHORITY

Mixture of central grant and local taxation systems
Traditional incremental budget

Traditional committee structure
Patron of service committee
Constituency role

Limited to scale of service provision and
priorities between services
Professionally-defined need;
centralised planning
Service departments

Limited; mediated by professions

Determined by economics of provision

Multi-tier system acceptable

Through members and committees

Inherent in professional service

DIAGRAM 6 (continued)

Characteristics of Process and Structure

THE MARKET-ORIENTED ENABLER

Financial implications

(i)	Basic source of revenue	Charging (community charge)
(ii)	Subsidiary sources of revenue	Leverage vis-a-vis private sector
		Local rating system

Political implications

(i)	Political management structures	Larger management board meeting regula◦
		Elected mayor?
(ii)	Key political roles	Board member
		Strategist, enabler, advocate

Organisational implications

(i)	Scope for authority-wide strategic planning	Local economic development emphasis (strategic parameter for market)
(ii)	Basis of service provision and planning	Market regulation emphasis and strong infrastructure planning
(iii)	Basis of internal organisation	Contract specification management and negotiation
		Strategic centre
(iv)	Approach to external relationships	Ring-holder for wide range of producer interests

Implications for Territorial structure

Unitary authority based on area of 'econo◦ identity' (e.g. journey to work catchment ◦

Implications for Accountability and Control

(i)	Main accountability link	Via local business interests
(ii)	Basis of control and inspection	Market regulation
		Maintenance of competition

THE COMMUNITY-ORIENTED ENABLER

Buoyant local revenue source (mix of rates/L.I.T.)
Needs-equalisation grant

Strong political executive plus area/neighbourhood
committees
Local representative strategy/policy-making
Advocacy/negotiation

Emphasis on community needs

Matrix organisation decentralised and (relatively)
de-professionalised and strategic centre
Strong decentralised offices

Strong, particularly to local people and
organisations to be influenced

Unitary authority or multi-tier system plus
requirement for decentralisation system

Via local community through participative democracy links
Citizen participation and power

DIAGRAM 6 (continued)

Characteristics of Process and Structure	THE SELF-SUFFICIENT AUTHORITY
Financial implications	
(i) Basic source of revenue	Buoyant local revenue source(mix of rates/L.I.T.)
(ii) Subsidiary sources of revenue	Needs-equalisation based on CG grant
Political implications	
(i) Political management structures	Strong political executive plus service committees
(ii) Key political roles	Strategy/policy-making service administration Casework Corporate Policy
Organisational implications	
(i) Scope for authority-wide strategic	High; emphasis on inter-service priorities planning
(ii) Basis of service provision and planning	Strong emphasis on service departments likely
(iii) Basis of internal organisation	Strong strategic centre
(iv) Approach to external relationships	Of limited importance but at discretion of L.A.
Implications for Territorial structure	Strong case for (relatively large) unitary authorities Minimal joint action
Implications for Accountability and Control	
(i) Main accountability link	Via the councillors through party/election mechanism
(ii) Basis of control and inspection	Inherent in professional service; internal performance review.

The implications of the ideal types for systems of local government

Diagram 6 sets out in summary form our assessment of the implications of each ideal type under five main headings - the implications for finance, political management, internal organisation, territorial structure and accountability processes. These implications are developed and discussed in subsequent paragraphs.

Implications for sources of finance

The system of local government finance should reflect the role and purpose of local government. Financial arguments should incorporate the basic principle that the more discretion or choice which local authorities are given in relation to policies and service standards, the more revenue should be raised from local sources rather than central grant (and vice versa). The residual authority would suggest a general emphasis on charging as the key element of resourcing. The community charge is (in principle at any rate) compatible with this approach to local government and would appropriately form the major source of revenue for local authorities supplementing revenue derived from services which were charged for directly. Although it is likely that a relatively small top-up of needs-equalisation-related central government grant would be needed, the main financial link would be the transaction between the local authority and its charge-payers, over the limited bundle of services provided by the residual authority. In the regulatory authority, the element of central grant would be proportionately larger reflecting the greater range of regulatory services provided (and the fact that they are provided indirectly rather than directly to local populations).

The two mechanisms of direct charging for services (where possible) and the use of the community charge would also figure prominently in the market-enabler authority. In this case there would be a further important aspect of local government finance to be considered. Leverage (the use of public funds to pump-prime or stimulate private sector investment which would not otherwise take place) is a key element of the market enabler role. The market enabler authority would clearly require a source of finance additional to the community charge (the logic of which does not fit with the broader development and planning role involved). A rating system (including industrial and commercial property) would have the benefit of recouping from the private sector some of the authority's investment in or for the area and would strengthen council and business links. This proposal would involve the abandonment of the uniform business rate, and the re-introduction of locally-determined business rates. The source of finance should clearly be local rather than central (although again some central grant for needs equalisation purposes might be needed) for the exercise of choice/discretion at the local level is by definition high under this option.

In the administrative agent authority, it would be logical for central grant to be the dominant feature of resource provision. This could be distributed either en bloc, on the basis of a detailed set of centrally-calculated relative needs assessment criteria, or (more logically) as a series of service-related specific grants allocated by the centre in response to local needs-based bids (cf. TPPS, HIPs). A relatively minor element of local fiscal autonomy to provide marginal enhancements of nationally-specified service standards would also be needed, either in the form of rates or local income tax.

The traditional mixture of central government grant and locally-raised revenue would be congruent with the community-oriented enabler and self-sufficient authority roles, with the balance logically in favour of the latter rather than the former, to reflect the high degree of local choice/discretion involved. A mixture of local rates and local income taxation would in principle be appropriate, to reflect the fact that services would be provided by the local authority to local businesses as well as local residents. The same broad principles apply to the traditional bureaucratic local authority, with the difference that in this ideal type, central government grant should logically provide a higher proportion of revenue.

Implications for political roles and management structures

The introduction provided a number of important role distinctions in considering the availability of discretion and control to local councillors. It distinguished between the operational role (of which sub-elements of strategy, policy-making and implementation, and organisational effectiveness were identified) and the representative role of which dimensions of local representative and representative for the authority as a whole were identified, in addition to the familiar party political representative role. Under our present voting system, the local representative role will remain an important element in the role repertoires of all councillors although the way it is interpreted will vary between different ideal types. All the other roles are, however, much more susceptible to variation, at least in relative emphasis.

The operational role, for example, changes significantly as one moves from one ideal type to another. The strategic role, on which the Audit Commission is placing increasing emphasis has only a limited significance in the regulatory and administrative agent authorities, and virtually none in the residual authority. The role increases in importance in the traditional bureaucratic authority (where it has typically been interpreted in terms of judging priorities between services) and in the market-oriented enabler (where its main emphasis would be upon economic development issues). Its significance is potentially strongest in the community-oriented enabler and self-sufficient authorities. That is not to say that even where the councillor's strategic role is potentially strong, the processes of strategic planning and management may not in reality be dominated (or led) by officers. Similar arguments about the scope and significance of the strategic role of councillors in the different types of authority apply also to the policy-making role.

The policy implementation (or administration) role, however, is of potential importance in all seven types of authority. It has been a major role emphasis for many councillors in the traditional bureaucratic authority (much to the increasing disapproval of the Audit Commission who advocate the familiar division of labour

71

between councillors/policy and officers/implementation; in fact the arguments are much more complex and subtle than this division would imply). A similar emphasis would also be likely in a self-sufficient authority. Given the paucity of other significant roles, it would be likely to be a major priority for councillors in the administrative agent authority. In the community-oriented enabler, it would be likely to operate through area/neighbourhood committees where it would become increasingly linked to the councillor's local representative role. In the three market-dominated types of authority there is little scope for councillor involvement in policy implementation/administration because of the reliance on contracts and the dominance of the client/contractor split.

The other major element of the operational role - the responsibility for organisational effectiveness - although relevant in different ways to each of the ideal types, is clearly more demanding in those types of authority with wider ambits of responsibility (market enabler, community enabler, self-sufficient authority and to a lesser extent traditional bureaucratic) than it is in those types of authority where the emphasis is upon managing or regulating a set of specific services. In the latter much of the impetus for organisational effectiveness stems from the basis on which the service delivery or regulatory units are organised. Given the increasing propensity for the decentralisation of responsibilities to cost-centres, the overall management task, although still significant is certainly less time-consuming (and again may in reality be more within the purview of the chief executive than the leading councillors). Certainly there is much less scope for councillor interference in the operational management of departments in those authorities where such decentralised procedures operate.

The councillor's external representative role (speaking for the area, through, for example, membership of other organisations) would be a particularly high-profile one in the two enabling ideal types (market and community), much less so in the other alternatives (although in relation to bidding for resources, there would be a role in each ideal type, especially perhaps in the specific-grant-dominated financial régime of the administrative agent). The local constituency representative role is in principle easier to operate in authorities which provide all (or most) of their services directly than those (for example, residual authority, market enabler) which work through contractors (particularly external contractors). In the latter situation the route to the solution of constituency problems is more difficult, operating through the client part of the organisation. The community enabler is the ideal type which would give the highest profile to the local representative role in a whole range of ways.

It is clear that the seven ideal types identified have different implications for the political management structure of the local authority. For the residual authority operating a limited range of services almost wholly through contracts, a small management board of councillors, meeting at most two or three times a year to agree specifications, let contracts, and receive monitoring reports is all that would be necessary. In the regulatory authority the scope for member activity would be greater (reflecting the greater range of responsibilities) but the scope for political choice would remain limited, and hence a small council (or board) meeting infrequently would also be appropriate.

An executive management board would also be appropriate to the 'market-oriented enabler' authority, but would in these circumstances be a much more powerful (and necessarily larger) political entity and might well co-opt external interests. It would, like the residual authority, have a key role in the specification, letting and monitoring of contracts, but would in addition play a proactive role in the development and operation of the economic development strategy emphasised in this ideal type. There would be a good deal of scope for an elected executive board (a stronger PLC model than that implied by the residual authority). The board would need to meet far more frequently than its counterpart in the residual authority.

In the case of the self-sufficient authority, with its wide range of tasks, its direct responsibility for providing services, and its strong emphasis on representative democracy (and the likely corollary of high political conflict), a two-tier governmental system of cabinet/representative assembly would be much more congruent (i.e. a Westminster model replicated at city/county level). However, the direct responsibility for service provision in this type of authority would also lend credence to the continuation of the familiar service committee structure (which was, and would remain, the major political management feature of the traditional bureaucratic ideal type).

A different type of two-tier political management system would be implied for the community enabler ideal type; a central executive with overall strategy and policy formulation and implementation responsibilities, and a set of area committees with considerable devolved powers, which would emphasise the representative role of the majority of council members. In both self-sufficiency and community enabler models, a relatively large number of councillors would be appropriate, compared with the relatively small numbers necessary to operate the residual and market enabler models.

Formal committees, emphasising administrative/implementation issues of service provision and the need of overall co-ordination and efficient use of resources would be an implied corollary of the administrative agent ideal type. There would be little need for a powerful political executive (personal or collective) or management board, because the scope for political choice in such an authority would be relatively narrow. The main activity of councillors would be in relation to casework and constituency matters, and in administering the rules.

Implications for management structures and processes

In the residual authority the basis of internal organisation would reflect the key tasks of contract-specification and contract-management (with clear organisational separation of client and contractor roles if the latter were retained within the authority). Except in large authorities, the distinction between (strategic) centre and client service department would become unnecessary. The minimal strategic/co-ordinative role of the centre could be combined with the contract specification and management role, with the whole (small) organisation operating in effect as the centre (any internal DSOs could appropriately be treated as arms-length quasi-companies linked only loosely with the centre). Contract specification and management would also be one of the key organisational bases of the market enabler but this type of authority would need a stronger, separate strategic centre (with pro-active enabling/networking and advocacy roles), and some kind of programme-area-based departmental structure, reflecting its greater range of service responsibilities and higher level of discretion in dealing with them (and the greater propensity for negotiation with external interests in each service area). For an equivalent population size, its number of directly employed staff would be significantly higher than the residual authority (although much lower than the other three options, or existing local authorities).

In the regulatory and administrative agent authorities, the professionally-based service department would be the dominant organisational feature. There would in each case be only a limited co-ordinating and budgetary-allocation role for the centre (but external inspection/regulatory procedures would be implied in each case, because of the detailed legislative basis of the services provided). Unlike the residual authority there would be no necessity for a formalised client/contractor separation in organisational terms. Indeed in the case of the administrative agent the scope for discretion within the client role (which would in effect have been taken out of the authority) would be so limited that to separate it out from the mechanics of service provision would seem pointless.

In the self-sufficient and traditional bureaucratic authorities, a strong emphasis on service departments (and committees) based on the major (professional-based) service areas (for example, education, housing, social services) would be expected in the organisational structure. In the self-sufficient authority, however, this service department and/or committee emphasis would be balanced by the need for a strong strategic centre to identify and prioritise community needs in a way which transcended departmental responsibilities, develop new initiatives to fill gaps, ensure that service departments co-ordinated their activities to meet strategic priorities and play a key role in the budgetary allocation process. In the traditional bureaucratic authority the strong strategic centre, carrying out this range of tasks was typically conspicuous by its absence (although it would not in principle be incompatible with this ideal type) and in particular budgetary processes normally operated on an incremental basis. In the community enabler, the appropriate principles of internal organisation would be decentralisation (in both political and task responsibility terms), matrix management, and the use of task forces (or project groups) based on inter-professional co-operation and public participation.

There would be important differences of external orientation within the management processes of the different types of authority. In the residual authority there would be very little need for such relationships (apart from relationships with contractors). In the market enabler, the external relations role would be much stronger, with the local authority best seen as ring-holder within a network of (primarily private sector) interests. The main external linkage for the administrative agent would be to central government (through its various departments predominantly at regional office level) and would be primarily responsive in style, though with an element of lobbying. In the regulatory authority there would be a similar emphasis (with a major role for professional associations as devices for information circulation and the maintenance of consistent performance standards). In the community enabler authority there would be an extremely wide network of external relations built around the central enabling role of the local authority itself; not just to local people, but also to local agencies (for example, private sector, other public sector and voluntary sector agencies) of all kinds. The need for extensive external relations in the self-sufficient authority would not necessarily be as strong, given the wide range of direct powers available to the authority. The emphasis would be a matter of local choice. In the weaker traditional bureaucratic version of self-sufficient authority, the need for extensive external relations was typically seen as limited, and was normally mediated by the professions, (although professions themselves are sustained by a network of legitimacy external to the authority).

Implications for territorial structure

Scale is in principle not significant for the residual authority and it is possible to postulate a relatively small authority (the Adam

Smith Institute suggests 50,000 population). Economies of scale are not relevant to the client role itself (with which the residual authority would be primarily concerned), because the responsibilities for client (service specification) and contractor (service provision) roles have been institutionally disengaged in this option. The authority merely has to specify the level of service it requires, and the market (or some other external agency) actually provides the service. Services which could not be operated at the small scale - police or fire for example - would be placed with central government, a special purpose quango or a joint authority. On the other hand the residual authority could be large; since it offers few services, being close to the consumer is not a consideration.

For the market enabler role, which emphasises the relationship of the local authority with local economic interests in seeking to strengthen the local economy, the appropriate basis of territorial definition for the local authority would be an area which had a logic of economic integration - travel to work areas or a distinctive economic catchment area. This would point towards much bigger territorial areas than those implied by the residual role, a solution which would have the advantage both of avoiding counterproductive effects of interauthority competition and of providing the authority with a strong enough resource base to negotiate effectively with the various external interests concerned. Such external interests would also involve not only central government but also the European Commission and local government interests in the rest of Europe. In this context the market enabler begins to imply a large and visible city region within a European Community of local democracy.

The key criterion of territorial structure for the administrative agent authority would be the efficiency of agency administration from Whitehall with the number and size of local units determined by the logistics of control from the centre (a Napoleonic model). The system would logically involve a system of single-purpose authorities each reflecting the most appropriate area for the service concerned. The regulatory model would follow the pattern of the residual model if the regulatory activity were to be contracted out. If on the other hand it was argued that regulation should take place in-house some economies of scale of regulation arguments would begin to apply.

Given the emphasis on direct service provision in the self-sufficiency model, economies of scale and professional conceptions of service delivery issues would also play a large part in considerations of territorial structure. If self-sufficiency, however, is to mean what it implies, then the whole range of local government services should presumably fall within the responsibility of a single tier of local government. The familiar unitary authority-based structure fits closely with the self-sufficiency philosophy. The joint board option for services is incompatible with the unitary principle, and the joint committee option inappropriate for services which are potentially politically contentious. For the traditional bureaucratic ideal type, the professional conceptions of service delivery and economies of scale arguments would also be relevant, but there would be less strong a case for a unitary authority and a two or multi-tier system would be more appropriate.

The community enabler role places great emphasis on the significance of local definitions of community. The scale at which the local community is perceived - neighbourhood or ward - is in general territorially too small to be feasible as the primary unit of government unless what is implied is a model of expanded parish councils (including urban parishes). A credible structural alternative for the community enabler would be the large unitary authority within which there would be a requirement to operate a scheme of devolved power to more parishes, communities or neighbourhoods.

Implications for accountability and review

There are two important issues to consider here. The first is the basis of the accountability processes linking the elected council with the population it serves. Although in each ideal type identified some form of representative democracy is assumed, the emphasis placed on the local election process varies from ideal type to ideal type. Secondly, we are concerned with the nature of the external review processes which are needed to safeguard the interests of local residents in relation to financial probity, consistency of decisions, and the three Es.

For the residual authority the main accountability link would be to the individual charge-payer (as customer). In the regulatory authority this form of accountability would be supplemented by an administrative form of accountability linked to the regulatory processes involved. For the market enabler, the idea of mutual responsibility or partnership, particularly between the council and the private sector, would best capture the nature of accountability processes. The private sector (typically through the local Chambers of Commerce and Trade) would certainly have a much more explicit presence in the accountability linkages involved in this option hence diluting democratic accountability.

For the community enabler, the major accountability link would be directly to local people, through their representation on and participation in area committees (and indeed in service provision itself). For the self-sufficient authority (as in the traditional bureaucratic authority) political accountability through the familiar electoral mechanisms would be emphasised. In the administrative agent authority, the key accountability linkage would be to Parliament and thereafter between aggrieved members of the public and internal or external review and appeal mechanisms (for example, Parliament, watch-dog bodies, or a local ombudsman). In parallel with these conceptions of accountability there would be an emphasis on market democracy (residual authority) participatory democracy (community enabler) and representative democracy (self-sufficient and traditional bureaucratic authorities) with the other ideal types proving less straightforward to categorise.

In principle, the greater the scope given to local authorities, the stronger the need for external review mechanisms. Although some provision for the three forms of administrative accountability - financial probity, administrative propriety and administrative efficiency - would be needed whatever ideal type were adopted, the closer one moves towards a strong emphasis on public provision/strong local government role the more wide-ranging one would expect such review mechanisms to be. Thus the administrative accountability role of the Audit Commission would be much more limited in the residual or regulatory authority than it would in the self-sufficient or community enabler models. The idea of a Quality Commission fits most logically within the administrative agent ideal type, though a strengthened Audit Commission or wider Local Government Commission would have a broader role in creating an inspection and accountability structure for models of local government much wider than the agent model.

Concluding comments

This section has drawn out some of the implications of the analytical framework used in the report for the current agenda of local government issues. A few issues remain undiscussed. One is the power of general competence. The ideal type with the strongest case for general competence powers is the self-sufficient authority. Quite apart from the scope such a power would give to act in a governmental capacity beyond the responsibilities to provide specific services sanctioned by legislation, there would be an important symbolic significance attached to the possession of a general competence power. The case is less strong, however, for the market or community enabler (and quite unnecessary for the residual or regulatory authority) given the emphasis within these ideal types on persuasion of other organisations to do things, rather than the authority itself carrying out the activity. In enabling authorities of this type, there is little reason to suppose that the kind of power currently possessed by local authorities to carry out activities for the benefit of its area (the old Section 137 powers) would not in itself give authorities the scope they needed, particularly if financial constraints were lifted. The ability of local authorities to undertake major initiatives beyond the scope of existing legislation could also be facilitated by a revival of their capacity to sponsor Acts of Parliament. It is in addition likely that a power of general competence would itself be circumscribed and that the effect might be to displace central/local conflict onto the question of which functions should be excluded from the general power. The importance of the general power lies in its symbolic value as a statement of the legitimacy and importance of local government as an institution. What is needed to sustain such legitimacy is political will and an improved central/local relationship - issues which a general power of competence would not in itself address.

A more significant question is that of the appropriate scope of service or functional responsibilities allocated to local government and the powers provided. The appropriate response to this issue will be a direct reflection of the ideological stance underpinning the ideal types identified earlier in this report. Any service which involves significant scope for political choice is in principle appropriate for governmental, rather than administrative, responsibility with regard to a particular range of decisions. There will be differences of view about the degree of political salience involved in a service (for example, police, fire, trading standards). For services that are regarded as politically salient, the issue is to what extent if any there is scope for local interpretation of national requirements or indeed whether the service is solely a matter for local determination. There is no way a study like this can demonstrate the desirability or otherwise of permitting local interpretive space (or powers of determination). It is very much a reflection of what civil society believes is the right balance of responsibilities between the public and private sectors, and within the public sector between central and local government responsibilities. Thus many services for which local authorities currently enjoy a degree of political choice (for example, education, housing) could, from certain ideological standpoints, be logically withdrawn from them. Alternatively services for which local authorities do not currently enjoy direct responsibility, such as employment training, the community aspects of health, water provision and sewerage and higher education could from different ideological standpoints legitimately be included within their range of responsibilities (as they have been in the past in Britain, and are at present in other countries). The evidence from elsewhere is again ambiguous; local government in other countries carries functions which British local government lacks whilst British local government holds responsibilities which in other countries do not rest with local government.

The distribution of powers relates to questions about levels and tiers and reintroduces the issue of regions and parishes.

These have not been discussed at length in this report save to point out that for some service responsibilities (strategic planning, highways, waste disposal, for example) a larger area may be appropriate. That area may be larger than current strategic authority (county) areas. Such large areas could co-exist with very small area authorities exercising minimal powers. The existence of possible variation in the appropriate levels of government, and the inherent tension between larger and smaller areas highlights the justification for a two or multi-tier system of government and the drawbacks to a unitary system.

In conclusion we return to the basic framework of analysis around which our research has been built - discretion and control - and the relative strength implicit in different models of local government.

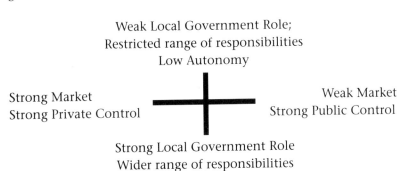

Weak Local Government Role;
Restricted range of responsibilities
Low Autonomy

Strong Market   Weak Market
Strong Private Control   Strong Public Control

Strong Local Government Role
Wider range of responsibilities
High Autonomy

Our findings are that different authorities occupy different positions in this space; individual authorities may well occupy different positions for different services. Recent history, however, has been of a general shift upwards and to the left (in the terms of the figure) as a consequence of a reduction and change in the functions of local government and a loss of local discretion and control. An insufficient resource base has been the cause of this shift at least as much as the loss of formal powers. This study supports the case that the justifications for local government (set out in Chapter 2) point to the desirability of a local government system which offers local authorities sufficient responsibilities and functions to allow them a choice as to where on the diagram they choose on political and administrative grounds to locate. Recent policy has forced authorities towards the top half of the diagram. Whilst authorities should be free to choose whether to locate high or low, right or left, the importance of keeping the bottom half of the diagram open and available must be stressed.

These general points form the basis of our serious concern about the way in which the current fundamental review of structure and finance is being carried out. This is not being done from the starting point of an analysis of, or choice between, various options which can be identified for the future role and purpose of local government. None of the three Consultation papers did this. Nor would a fundamental review operating from this starting point be possible in the time period the government have set aside for it. The desire to link considerations of local government finance and structure is commendable but there is a real danger that given the political importance of developing an alternative to the community charge, a thorough investigation of more fundamental issues has been precluded. It is already clear that one of the effects of the 1991 budget proposals and the direct financing by central government of further education and sixth form colleges has had the effect of reducing substantially the proportion of local government finance which is raised locally. The change has profound implications for the role and purpose of local government (it implies for example a de facto move towards the administrative agent ideal type). Yet the implications for education, or for local government as a whole have not been properly understood, let alone debated.

In the light of the unprecedented level of recent piecemeal change in the structure and operations of local government, and the level of uncertainty engendered by the weight and scope of the change, it is clear to us that a much more fundamental and informed review of local government than could possibly be provided by the Heseltine review is required at this particular point in its history. If a departmental committee of inquiry was needed in 1985 to examine the role of politics in local government (the Widdicombe Committee, which sat for over a year and commissioned in the process an impressive programme of original research) then how much greater is the need for a similar committee of inquiry (or indeed Royal Commission) to look at the linked issues of finance, functions, structure and central-local relations from the starting-point of a clarification of the role and purpose of local government. We have already made clear the limits to what can be achieved in the kind of research programme we are reporting on here. But we are clear that the kind of questions we have raised and process of analysis we have undertaken could and should be considered much more thoroughly and in much greater detail than we have been able to do.